Preventing Sexual Abuse in Congregations

A Resource for Leaders

Karen A. McClintock

Herndon, Virginia

www.alban.org

Scripture quotations, unless otherwise noted, are from the New Revised Standard Version of the Bible, copyright © 1989, Division of Christian Education of the National Council of the Churches of Christ in the United States of American and are used by permission.

Cover design: Adele Robey, Phoenix Design

Library of Congress Cataloging-in-Publication Data

McClintock, Karen A., 1953-
Preventing sexual abuse in congregations : a resource for leaders / Karen A. McClintock.
p. cm.
Includes bibliographical references.
ISBN 1-56699-295-8
1. Pastoral theology. 2. Sex crimes—Prevention. 3. Sexual harassment—Prevention. I. Title.

BV4011.3.M33 2004
261.8'3272—dc22

2004010342

08 07 06 05 04 VG 1 2 3 4 5 6 7 8 9 10

CONTENTS

Dedication

Written in gratitude for the life and faith of

Alene Dorcas Felder

1918–2003

FOREWORD

Those of us who work at picking up the pieces in shattered congregations have also spilled quite a bit of ink writing about recovery in the aftermath of clergy trust betrayals. However, we have not had a good resource that aims squarely at prevention in the congregation. And so it is with great pleasure that I write the foreword to this very timely and much-needed resource.

Because Karen McClintock writes out of the depth of her own considerable experience, she is able to deliver wise advice about all the obstacles that hinder the congregation's ability to engage in healthy relationships while also being in community. Strategies for shame reduction, releasing the stranglehold of secrets, discerning what constitutes respectful and nurturing touch, coping with addictive behaviors, and creating safety in counseling settings are all here, and McClintock's approach avoids the extremes of either establishing rigid rules or just muddling through.

I would go so far as to say that we risk being seriously negligent if we do not fully embrace the task of preventing sexual abuse in our faith communities. Furthermore, we can provide a model for the rest of the culture, which at this time seems hopelessly entangled in a toxic mix of sexual repression and obsession. This lively, frank, and compelling book will make the task much easier.

Both the content and the design of this book offer very accessible descriptions of all the common dilemmas, occasions for personal reflection, suggestions for group work, and good examples of policies and procedures. The dynamic of gradual creep is also fully described and explained, and clergy, seminarians, congregants, and judicatory officials who read this book may be much more likely to heed any warning flags well ahead of the storm. Each chapter addresses a topic that leaders and congregants can examine in depth.

Prevention of sexual abuse requires that certain steps be taken, and there is a logical order in which they generally need to occur. The first step is often overcoming the massive inertia and shame that most of us carry around—regarding not only issues of sexuality, but also issues of abuse of power. The two are so intertwined as to be hard to tease apart, and one often masks the other. If we remind ourselves that doing nothing is also making a decision, it may be easier to take that most difficult first step, even if we know that it is inevitable that some people in the congregation will try to block the initiative before it is even more than a gleam in someone's eye.

Although we can reasonably anticipate significant resistance to this discussion, I see another use for this book: it can serve as a major tool of recovery for congregations that have incidences of serious leadership abuse *anywhere* in their pasts, even when the abuse has not been overtly sexual in nature. We have learned that overt sexual abuse in a congregation is usually just the tip of the abuse iceberg. Intimidation, harassment, emotional abuse, a rigid and arbitrary leadership style, withdrawal into gradual isolation, all seem to be highly damaging "fellow travelers" in such settings.

When abuse happens in the context of a faith community, it often develops gradually, so that people lose their ability to see and name what is going on. Perpetrators are often adept at sending very mixed signals, and paradoxically, the offender often is charismatic and one on whom people easily become dependent. Confusion becomes the order of the day, and the silence and repression required to keep the blinders on can gradually creep into the entire system. Often, laity in these settings believe they, too, have permission to be abusive. Then a congregation may be set up to experience a string of multiple abuses of power from lay or clerical leaders well after the original, perhaps even forgotten, traumatic event. The resulting culture of abuse sets the community up for a massive crisis when an offender is finally removed. Therefore, any time we gain entry into a recently traumatized congregation, not only is serious recovery work indicated, but preventive work must surely follow.

As with the task of abuse prevention, however, recovery entails a developmental process. First, people need to be given information, education, and then plenty of time to grieve their losses, however these are experienced. Then they must begin the arduous process of reestablishing trust at all levels of the congregation. This takes far more time and effort than many are willing to give, but it cannot be rushed, and time spent on the front end will yield great dividends later on. Once these tasks are accomplished, a gradual readiness to take the longer and deeper look at the quality of communal life will emerge. I believe every congregation in recovery would benefit from a careful study of all the issues that surround sexuality, using this book as the text to guide that study.

This book is an invaluable tool, therefore, not only for those who want to apply it purely as a prevention measure, but also for those who want to put the crowning touch to a well-designed recovery process after any kind of serious power abuse has taken place. In fact, there is a short period in a congregation's development following a major crisis when the attention of congregants is riveted on the recent traumatic events. In spite of the current upheaval, leaders are often presented with a perfect opportunity to bring about major and lasting change in a system that may have slowly closed in on itself, with disastrous results. The opportunity should not be squandered.

Even as we undertake this often difficult journey, we need to be gentle with ourselves and others as we explore together the deep scars that many of us carry. Because dealing with issues of sexuality takes a lot of psychic energy, I would advise going slowly and giving people enough time to absorb the information and its effect on them in a context of care and support. A retreat setting with opportunities to take walks, talk informally, and laugh at the absurdity of it all would help.

As a people set in a certain time and culture, we all carry some of the scars collectively. The twin journeys of prevention and recovery are well worth going on together.

Nancy Myer Hopkins

PREFACE

Are you ready to abuse-proof your congregation? If one child or adult is spared the confusing ordeal of enduring unwanted touch, it will be worth your time to read this book. If you, having read this book, notice some impropriety and speak up about it right away, you may stop a child or adult parishioner from victimization. You may be able to prevent a pastoral marriage from ending. You may avoid a congregational scandal that leads to a decline in the vitality and membership of your congregation. Whether you are a pastor, a lay person, or a student preparing for ministry, you can be more aware of the dangers that are inherent in pastoral ministry and alert to the risks of sexual boundary crossings.

Sexual abuse in congregations is preventable. It does not happen in a vacuum; it happens in a system. Within that system, secrecy, shame, and silence can foster a climate of permission for sexual boundary violations. Theological perspectives can deepen shame and create an environment where people act out. Within congregations the subject of sexuality has been taboo, yet all around us today in the media and popular culture, taboo breaking is glorified with attention and curiosity. Recent media presentations about the sexual abuse of children in the church have played upon our fascination with human sexuality. Religions no longer hold the last word on sexual morality. However, that does not mean that we should let the popular media and culture take charge of our sexual ethics. Within the pages of this book are concrete suggestions to bring sexuality and sexual issues into congregational life. We will either do that consciously or continue to see the damage of sexual abuse.

One congregation hired three pastors in a row who crossed sexual boundaries with parishioners. One pastor after another committed sexual harassment and abuse. After the first one, the people concluded that, "He had a problem." They removed him, thinking that the problem would go away. It did not. The next pastor they hired crossed a sexual boundary as well. They thought it was a strange coincidence, fired her, and called another pastor. When the third pastor violated a child, they could no longer pretend that it was just a problem with those individuals, and they started to evaluate their own part in the abuse. Was it their willingness to ignore the signs that their pastor was burned out? Were they hiring a certain type of charismatic leader who was particularly seductive? Why didn't anyone notice the pastors' behaviors before they became harmful? Had they trusted their pastors too much? Was there full and complete healing from the damage of the first pastor by open discussion about it and about the short- and long-term consequences of it? What combination of factors led to these damaging abuses? These are some of the questions that will be explored in this resource.

You are invited to join in making your congregation a community that is safe for everyone. Part of that invitation is that you begin to talk about sex and sexuality. At first, this will seem awkward and unnerving. Depending on your culture and background, you were likely taught to keep sexual subjects private. You may have been taught to fear sexuality, either for its unbridled passion or for its sinfulness. It is my hope that when you read this book, the subject of sex will become more and more normal. This resource affirms the goodness and pleasure of human sexuality while also addressing its distortions.

My approach to the topic of sexual abuse in the church follows Jesus' witness that we be people of grace and truth. In the early 1990s, when my denomination began offering workshops on sexual boundary issues, I was trained to be a leader for one of them. Our message to clergy was legalistic and moralistic. We got together and laid out the rules and the consequences, as parents do with adolescents. You can imagine what ensued after that. Rule breaking. We learned that shame-based education was ineffective.

Ten years later, when I was asked to provide training for hundreds of clergy and laity, I decided to take a clearly different approach. I am glad to share this new model with you. Areas of abuse that you will find addressed in this book include clergy and laity adult sexual boundary violations, child abuse, and sexual and gender harassment. While there are guidelines to follow in the contents of this book, laying down rules is not the goal. The goal is to offer grace and safety through open dialogue and decisive action.

When you have finished this book, you will be familiar with conditions in parishes and in the mental health of individuals within them that lead to risky behaviors. Not all of the violations in congregations are between clergy and parishioners. Sometimes members of the congregation sexually harass their pastors or other members of the congregation. Lay staff members are often at risk of boundary violations with members of congregations. And sometimes people who come to worship or to the congregation have unhealed wounds that make them vulnerable to, or even solicitous of, violation.

When you have finished this book you will be equipped to recognize and set sexual boundaries for yourself and to open dialogue about these issues in your congregation. You will have laughed at, celebrated, and honored human sexual power, pleasure, and vulnerability. You will have gained the knowledge you need, and perhaps the courage, to communicate these ideas within your congregation so that children and vulnerable adults are protected.

When people visit a new congregation, they take in many messages. Some are clear, like the printed data in a bulletin, or the words spoken by the liturgist and preacher. But there are other messages, too. The congregation sends out messages by the way it welcomes new people, by the touching that goes on in worship, and by the intuitive feeling of wellness that can be found in a congregation that has carefully integrated safety and respect into its everyday life. In a congregation that is ashamed of sexual indiscretions, has unhealed wounds, or has secrets within it, people get an uncomfortable feeling when they worship there. You may have visited a place like this yourself.

By contrast, in communities of faith where sexuality issues are neither repressed nor flaunted, people intuitively feel comfortable. Joy and laughter are easily expressed and people are given permission to touch or to keep personal distance without any concern for uniformity.

I worship in a congregation that includes sexuality issues in its daily life. This was not always the case, and one pastor in the church's history was fired, in part due to issues about sexuality. During that time, the congregation was diminished in size and spirit. But 15 years later, with new leadership and healing, the congregation integrates sexuality in its life in such an easy and subtle way that outsiders may not even notice it. The congregation communicates that it is respectful, joyful, and alive.

What kinds of things are they doing? The youth group had a retreat where a medical doctor, a social worker, and a pastor led them through two days of discussion about human sexuality issues. Parents gathered for a one-day seminar on how to talk to children about sexuality. The pastor is open in sermons about love and about passion and uses language that unabashedly shows that he celebrates all aspects of life. I distinctly remember one Sunday when he invited people forward for communion and said to the congregation, "Come to this table as you are, bring your whole naked self." I had no previous memory of ever hearing the word *naked* in church but I found it both thought provoking and healthy.

I am not advocating that we all become nudists at church! I am advocating that we replace our fear of sexual words, that we use them in expressing our life with God who knows us and celebrates our sexuality, and that we shape communities where both safety and sexuality are topics of regular attention.

This book is offered so that you and your congregation can find ways to protect the children and vulnerable adults in your midst and in your community. It is offered so that fewer and fewer clergy are discouraged by harassment, or fired for speaking up about a truth in the life of the church "family" secret that has been hidden for a long, long time. I hope that clergy families are strengthened by the book as they become aware of the occupational and emotional risks inherent in pastoral ministry. It is offered because of the acute and long-term damage of sexual abuse on individuals, families, and congregations. This damage can be prevented.

Acknowledgments

My appreciation is extended to Beth Gaede of the Alban Institute for her thorough and creative editorial work, and to Jean Semrau and Judith Sanford for their editorial contributions. I also want to thank the women with whom I write every week: Joan, Ann, Liz, Alice, and Marcy. They keep me honest, inspire my writing, and provide enduring love and strength so that I can continue this work. I acknowledge the grace-filled love of God about whom I will write my whole life and still only begin to describe. Lastly, this book is written so that many who have been injured by harassment or abuse in congregations or elsewhere will find hope in our efforts to prevent any further damage.

ONE

Abuse Prevention

We have an epidemic of sexual abuse in the church in this decade. We can no longer avoid these issues. Plenty of resources are available to look at what to do when damage occurs from sexual boundary violations or sexual abuse. This book is about how to prevent that damage.

Across 20 years as a parish pastor, no experience was more frightening and disconcerting to me than what took place one Christmas Eve as the congregation was leaving the sanctuary. A married man in one of my parishes stroked my hand and told me, "You look beautiful in candlelight." This was the beginning of a series of harassing comments and behaviors that I was ill prepared to deal with. Ignorance and naïveté on my part and in the parish contributed to the problem escalating.

Other pastors have encountered even more debilitating harassment and abuse. While I was writing this book, I learned about numerous stories of this nature. One parish I'm acquainted with has been dealing with a church visitor who is stalking their pastor—a situation they have had to handle without a guidebook or resource such as this.

A youth director in another congregation has been charged with sexual harassment by a teen who was alone in a car with him. The situation is the classic problem of "his word against hers." The problem would not have arisen if he had refused to drive a teen home alone in his car. The situation could have been prevented.

Other, similar stories have come to my attention: An overly friendly usher learned that he could have been accused of sexually harassing visitors. A pastor who disclosed too much about his own sexual life has been charged with sexual harassment. A pastor on a home visit encountered a naked man with a lot of pornography. A registered sex offender, whose pastor was the only one aware of his history, was arrested on new charges.

These stories place a human face on sexual abuse. Sexual boundary violations, sexual abuse, and allegations of misconduct could happen to any of us, at any time. What can we learn from these devastating circumstances and near-misses? How can congregations prepare themselves to handle these kinds of situations when they arise? The goal is to avoid disastrous situations where sexual harassment or abuse are likely to occur. Some of the stories are tragic, some a bit comical, and all of them illustrate the need for education and compassion. They are recounted here so that we can catch the human errors that lie within them and learn from them.

My personal passion about sex abuse prevention arises from my experiences with sexuality issues in the church. As a child I was raised in a family with sexual secrets, and I know the ways that secrets harm families and church families. As a United Methodist pastor I endured sexual harassment that reduced my effectiveness in ministry and inhibited church growth. As a single pastor, I live with the inevitable tension between the pleasure of my sexuality and professional restrictions on its expression. As a clinical psychologist I encounter people with many kinds of sexual wounds. My clients teach me healing and the power of a resurrected life. Along the way we learn some things that could have prevented these wounds in the first place.

All of the stories in this book are approximations of true stories. One of my ethical principles is to never disclose people's stories in such a way that they would be recognizable. Names, genders, cultural issues, and other data are changed so that we can understand the essence of these true stories without breaking confidences.

What We've Tried That Hasn't Worked

People of faith and goodwill have been aware of sexual abuse in congregations for years. Why hasn't it been eradicated? A close look at the problems shows us that congregations have tried to various solutions, to no avail. Old ways that have failed to prevent sex abuse include silence, power, repression, avoidance, and shame. This chapter deals with each of these in turn. Remember the old saying that a fool is a person who tries the same thing over and over again hoping for different results? Call it foolishness, call it ignorance, call it bad habits—congregations have clearly been ineffective in addressing the problem of sex abuse.

This is a book that provides new alternatives. The subject is hard to handle, so I want you to feel empowered rather than bogged down in old mindsets. I'm going to list things that haven't worked first, ever so briefly, so that we can name these old approaches and leave them behind. Then we'll be ready to clear new paths in the prevention of sexual abuse.

> ***For Personal Reflection***
>
> What situations of sexual abuse have arisen in congregations you know? How were those situations handled? How could they have been handled differently? What has been the lasting effect of those incidents on the individuals involved and the congregation?

"Shhhhh!!!!!"—The Problem of Silence

Treating the whole subject of sex and particularly sexual abuse as if it's "off limits" has not stopped pastors and laity from abusing children and vulnerable adults. Individuals living with the pain of abuse are sitting among us in worship, at Bible studies, and in other activities. The "shhhh" method has kept these victims and witnesses of their abuse silent. These individuals have wisdom from which we can learn, but we have often joined them in keeping silent. Those who have been wounded by abuse are doubly wounded by silence. We have an obligation to listen to them and to let them teach us.

We're at a time when more and more people are talking about their own abuse. Where once the words of women and children were ignored, they are beginning to be heard. Men who have been silent about their own victimization are also speaking out. The voices of all these victims demand that we develop safer congregations.

Remember the "think no evil, see no evil, hear no evil" monkeys? People of faith have tried to address sexuality like these monkeys. When it comes to sex abuse it's the silence, the looking the other way, and the refusal to hear the voices of the people directly involved that has increased the prevalence of abuse. It hasn't helped the victims, the perpetrators, or our congregations to be so hush-hush about the whole topic. We are in a climate of increasing openness and congregations can either lag behind or seize this new opportunity to see, hear, and speak up.

One way to speak up is to provide training and education for children, youth, and adults about safe touching and dangerous touching. Congregations that place the topic of sex in the curriculum are saying, "We choose education over ignorance." The time to keep everyone in the dark on issues of sexual harassment and sexual assault is now over. Once Sunday school children have been taught to speak up, they will protect themselves by enlisting the help of trained adults. Once they use words to set boundaries, learn how to say no to unwanted or aggressive behavior from other children and adults, problem behaviors will be addressed and stopped. When children talk to their parents and to trusted adults about uncomfortable touches and feelings, and when adults honor their stories, we will be victorious in stopping abuse.

"I'm Entitled"—The Problem of Power

Denominations and congregations have dealt with sexuality issues by giving the job of monitoring and regulating sexuality to pastors, theologians, and others in positions of authority. This has led to the thought that it is appropriate for church leaders to take the helm in decisions about the sexual activities of others. This is an attempt to limit the negative consequences of sexual activity, yet because of the predominance of male power and authority within the tradition it has led to different rules and consequences for others depending on gender, class, and sexual orientation.

While some well-intentioned people in religious traditions have used this power wisely, we know of far too many instances when they have not. Especially when the person in authority feels entitled to favors (some of them sexual), an abuse of power is the end result. Too often we find that influential people use that influence to gain sexual access.

People in power have used their privileged positions to behave as they pleased with people in the parish, and too many bystanders have supported them in their sense of entitlement. One of the manifestations of this entitled feeling can include demands for sexual favors. Entitlement leads to the abuse of power, one form of which is sexual and includes harassment, molestation, and sexual assault. To prevent sexual abuse, an honest appraisal of the power dynamics in the congregation is essential. The inappropriate use of power needs to be named and stopped.

It's a new day and the church is up against huge challenges. Media reports that discredit clergy serve a helpful function in society if they reduce the deification of these leadership positions. When we name abuses of power, and the power embedded in the tradition, we reduce the possibility of sexual abuse.

For Personal Reflection

When have you experienced people in power or authority using their position to gain sexual favors? Who was harmed by that behavior? What does your religious tradition say about protecting those who are vulnerable or less powerful?

"Not Me"—The Problem of Repression

One way that religious authorities have attempted to solve sexual problems is by repression. Repression is not just keeping silent about sexuality; it's pushing down or denying sexual fantasies, attractions, and activities in oneself and others. This is a way that people attempt to control the frequency of sex, the purpose of sex, the positions used, the methods of preventing pregnancy and transmittal of sexually transmitted diseases, and moral issues related to the consequences of sex, including pregnancy. Religious authorities have selected the definitions of sexual "sin," including who gets to engage in it and who doesn't.

Various attempts to limit sexuality have backfired. Repression involves a denial of one's instinctive desires (the thoughts you have) and drives (the action taken based on those thoughts). Repression has failed to control the sexuality of clergy or others in congregations. The more a person tries to repress sexual desires and to limit impulses toward a desired partner, the more those desires push their way into conscious action.

Clergy in particular have been held to high standards for sexual behavior. They have often been forbidden from acknowledging their own sexuality, even in confidential settings. Clergy repression has contributed to the breaking of rules and to acting out behavior. Both clergy and laity have been taught by puritan ancestors to deal with sexuality in this repressed way. What those ancestors didn't know is that subjects that are considered taboo are more exciting, and become even more of a focus for people's thoughts and feelings.

We need to find a balance between the repression of the past and a no-holds-barred permissive present. Defining and refining sexual ethics can provide this balance. Throughout this book we will look at professional ethics as a way to acknowledge sexual issues as they arise and to examine ways to eliminate or minimize the physical and emotional damages of inappropriate sexual behavior.

"It's No Big Deal!"—The Problem of Avoidance

It hasn't worked to pretend that sex is neutral. While sex is driven biologically, as I will talk about later in this chapter, sex is not *only* a biological activity. The physical arousal system, the emotional system, the soul, and the mind are all connected. Sexual activity affects one's spiritual well-being and has psychological consequences. Trying to separate sex from these other aspects of the self is ludicrous. Yet we have been trying to do that since the early Gnostic teachings that separated the body from the soul.

The topic of sexuality is broad and encompasses the search for loving relationships. It's the source of our jokes, the aim of our flirtations, and a confounding issue that drives us into therapy. Sex has moved out of the bedroom. Conversations about sex are all around us—in the board room, the living room, the locker room (nothing new there). Sex is talked about in every space we inhabit—except the sanctuary. The only place it hasn't become the main topic seems to be at church! I think it's time to change that. Roughly 50 percent of Americans live as singles or in committed partnerships and are not legally married. Many young people are sexually active. If our congregations do not engage with these people in ways that are affirming and respectful of their sexual choices, we will continue to lose the opportunity to be in fellowship with them.

"It's Disgusting!"—The Problem of Shame

Congregations have attempted to keep sexual behavior in line through the use of individual and community shame. Shame is connected to feelings of disgust and unworthiness. Where do we get the notion that sex is dirty? Some of us learned this from parents at home; others learned it at church. Some of us heard our preachers say that sexual fantasies, masturbation, and sexual experiences outside of marriage make us unworthy and disgusting in the sight of God. Wherever we learned it, we need to question it. Isn't sex a God-given gift?

We've tried to stop many kinds of sexual activities by slinging shame at sex itself and at those who engage in it. Words like *immoral, degenerate,* and *perverted* reinforce shame. Old words that are out of common usage describe sexual shame, words like *abomination.* The shame lexicon includes contemporary words such as *slut* and *whore.* I am convinced that shame is part of the problem, not the cure. The more shame a person feels about his or her sexuality, the more distortions of its goodness are likely to arise.[1]

Sex abuse prevention in the church begins with the elimination of individual and community-based shame. This involves education about ethical sexuality that reduces dichotomous thinking and increases value-centered decision making. It involves freeing perpetrators and victims of sex abuse from debilitating condemnation. This requires a viewpoint wherein we separate each individual's worth in the sight of God from his or her behaviors. Sexual behavior changes across the life span. Damaging sexual behaviors can be addressed and healed more effectively without shame. Grace is the only cure for shame, and in this resource we will learn to use grace to prevent sex abuse.

This concludes our review of some prior attempts to prevent sex abuse. Knowing what hasn't worked in the past prepares us to take a new and different approach in the present. As you continue through the book you will find that old, ineffective strategies are replaced with new ones. In prevention we leave behind the old ways of silence, power, repression, avoidance, and shame. What we will learn instead is to speak out, share power, take responsibility, celebrate sexuality, and offer grace. As we continue to explore the problems, new solutions will be our focus.

> *For Personal Reflection*
>
> When have you felt ashamed or embarrassed by a reference to sexuality at church? How did you and the congregation respond? How often have you heard sermons that include sexual themes and topics? Where these experiences positive? If not, why not?

Four Guiding Principles

This book is based on four guiding principles about sex. They are that sex is powerful, relational, situational, and complex. In describing each of these areas, I will show that there is both goodness and danger in each aspect of sex. As you consider the blessings and challenges of sexuality, I will show you ways to increase the blessings and to decrease the potential for damage.

Sex is a lot like cooking. Let me explain. I cook without recipes most of the time. I throw a bunch of stuff together and see what happens. Usually the results are pretty good. But throw in any wrong ingredient—say turmeric or cayenne pepper in a mild cream sauce—and the whole thing can become a disaster. It seems to me that sexuality is like this. It takes wonderful ingredients such as safety, honor, mutuality, and respect to make up a good sexual experience. But there are a few ingredients that, when they are added in, create disastrous outcomes. Take sex and add in manipulation, power, addiction, or aggression and it quickly becomes repugnant.

The guiding principles help us to separate out the elements that make a sexual experience holy and wonderful from those that make it demeaning, degrading, and have the potential for long-term damage to individuals and whole congregations.

Sex Is Powerful

We have been made in God's image. The Hebrew scriptures are clear that God's image is both male and female (Gen. 1:27). Our sense of gender and our sexual attractions and drives make up a large portion of our identity. Our sexual experiences and relationships define the essence of our core sense of self. No wonder sex is so powerful.

There are a lot of ways that sex is good for us and works to our benefit—emotionally, spiritually, and biologically. We have less control over our sexual arousal and attraction than we'd like to think. In sexual activity it is not only the actions themselves, but the meaning we derive from them that makes them so vital. One person may interpret a flirtatious encounter as only a flirtatious encounter, while another may interpret the same encounter as the beginning of love. What meaning do we attribute to our own physiological arousal? If we misinterpret a physiological state as psychological love, or vice versa, then trouble arises.

It is precisely the power of sex that leads to its misuses. The wonderful power of our body's responses can certainly be confusing. When we feel aroused in an inappropriate moment, or attracted to some forbidden partner, we may mistake this for love, and with this interpretation we feel more inclined to pursue the relationship. The presence of restrictions and taboos on a relationship that is very appealing increases the desire for sex. If we send signals to our brain that this partner is the one with whom to mate, the brain starts producing biochemicals that propel us deeper into the relationship.

When God looked out upon the earth and saw that every created thing was good, this surely included the playful sexual desires and behaviors of every species. God could have made it possible for us to reproduce without so much pleasure in it. Some animals do it on the fly, some never even touch each other, some of them devour their partner afterward. But as humans we have been given the extraordinary gift of pleasure. We have been given the capacity for great sexual ecstasy as well as the responsibility to use it consciously, and for the greatest good.

We are all capable of desire. This desire involves our spiritual yearning, our relational yearning, and our biological hardwiring. These desires often lead us to sex, because so many of our needs can be met in a sexual exchange; for example, the need to be comforted, cherished, and to engage in pleasurable contact with a loving partner. The desire to pleasure one another is an expression of loving intimacy. Orgasmic sex can raise moods, stimulate clarity of thought, and increase the body's immune system. If you want to stay healthy, slip right up next to your sweetheart and say, "Honey, I feel a cold coming on. Let's have sex tonight!" Or, get the same effect through masturbation. An orgasm provides the body with a rush of pain-killing chemicals that can decrease the achy feelings that accompany your cold.

Sexual arousal is part of the parasympathetic autonomic nervous system. When a person shifts from a highly anxious state, such as fight, flight, or freeze, and into a state of calm, the body interprets this as preparation for sexual arousal.[2] In meditation the body may flood with a sense of aliveness that is stimulating. The spiritual teachings of many traditions have spoken of the sexual high that accompanies total relaxation. Meditation techniques target the state of trance that can lead to this response. Mystics who wrote erotically about God may have been feeling quite pleasantly titillated.

The body and the soul are intricately connected. Sex can be good for your spiritual health. Sex can put you in touch with the holy, and it can heal past injuries to the body and the soul. Our bodies store memories of prior touch and prior sexual encounters and these affect our self-esteem and our sense of being at one with God. If the shame-filled messages of our parents or religious tradition condemn us for a prior sexual experience, we may feel irreparably damaged. The healing of this damage is a spiritual process of accepting God's grace and love, and then replacing the traumatic experiences with positive experiences with loving human partners. People who have survived sexual traumas such as child molestation or rape can be healed by loving partners and by learning safe and graduated touch techniques to help them regain trust and experience pleasure.

For Personal Reflection

How, for you, are sexuality and spirituality connected? Think of some sexual experiences that have been hurtful to you. Think of some that have been healing. What were the differences between the hurtful and healing sexual experiences?

One Sunday when I had preached about sexuality a senior member of the congregation took me aside. He said, "I want to tell you about a prayer that my wife and I pray together before having sex." This piqued my interest, so we stepped aside in the foyer for a little more privacy, and he told me his prayer. Surprisingly, I had learned this prayer as a table grace. "Lord, for what we are about to receive, make us truly thankful."

This man and his wife obviously knew how to connect sexuality and the spiritual practice of gratitude.

A friend of mine once commented that "sexuality is the place where worship and play intersect." Many individuals and couples believe that their sexual expression is a holy sacrament. The sacredness of any ritual is viewed in the soul of the participant. In Jewish tradition there is an expectation that the rabbi and his or her spouse will have sexual relations on the Sabbath. This keeps the Sabbath holy and their relationship holy.

Mystics have likened their relationship to Christ to the bonding of husband and wife. The church has called itself "the bride of Christ." Erotic literature is embedded in every religious tradition. In many cultures the ultimate way to be holy or to be in the presence of the holiness is through sexual intimacy. I recently asked 100 people, "How many of you can separate your sexuality from your spirituality?" Not a single hand was raised.

There is no area of life that is not affected by our sexuality. If we continue to assert that it can be separated from our sacramental faith we will have fostered a climate of repression and acting out. Prevention entails individuals and congregations reclaiming sexuality as the soulfully good thing that it is.

Sex Is Relational

From the first flirtatious moment, to the steady relationship, to the years after the honeymoon, chemicals in the brain are activated and driving us toward a partner.

During courtship the body produces ample supplies of several substances that pull us toward one another. They are the chemicals of attraction. We are drawn together by chemicals that are subtly transmitted via body odor, skin secretions, and breath. Remember back when everyone was wearing musk oils and fragrances to draw in their mates? Perfume companies are now trying to replicate the more recently discovered biochemicals called pheromones. These chemicals are fired off when a desirable mate is within range, and are believed to increase in power when a biochemical collision takes place between two people at the same time. Pheromones peak at the beginning of courtship and wane between 12 and 18 months. When people say, "The honeymoon is over," they may be experiencing a very real drop in the level of attraction chemicals that first led them to mate.

These biologically driven highs can be so powerful that they contribute to sexual addiction, according to Pat Carnes, psychologist, author, and founder of the Meadows Institute in Wickenberg, Arizona. "Beyond the pleasurability of love, there also exists the 'rush' or intoxication experience during the attraction stage of new love."[3] The good gift of this physical and emotional intoxication is at the root of why we both crave and fear sex.

Using animal subjects, Michael Liebowitz, author of *The Chemistry of Love,* found that another biochemical called phenylethylamine (PEA) in high concentrations increased sexual arousal and erotic behavior in monkeys when other monkeys were present. The object of sexual interest awakened the response of the monkeys to the chemical.[4] In other words, this biochemical prefers that you have sex in the company of someone else.

Bonding chemicals are also released in the body when we experience orgasm with someone. (These are likely the same chemicals that appear to be limited or absent in children with autism.) When oxytocin is released in the body, wonderful feelings of being connected to one's partner are released.[5] This is why people who have casual sex sometimes confuse the experience with love. They "feel" bonded. For example, a friend of yours goes out on Friday night and picks up an unappealing but available stranger. The two of them have orgasmic sex. The next morning your friend thinks that this unappealing partner is the gorgeous cat's meow. Like it or not, they've bonded.

This is also why couples who stop having sex experience a deterioration of the feeling of being connected to each other. The apostle Paul indicated that it was not good for husbands and wives to be away from each other for very long, even if they were in prayer, on spiritual retreat, or fasting. He may have been aware of the bonding power of sex, if not the biochemistry of the bonding. Sex is like a biochemical glue that holds relationships together.

The Danger of Biochemicals. While all of these good things happen during courtship, dating, and first sexual encounters, there are dangerous aspects to the biochemical pulls of sexuality. These include the arousing combination of sex and fear. When people feel they are doing something considered bad or crossing into forbidden territory, their level of fear goes up and so does their level of arousal.

Physiological studies in human subjects have found that these feel-good chemicals are even more prevalent when individuals feel a sense of fear about the activity. The breaking of a taboo creates additional anxiety, and the adrenaline rush of it is similar to what is known as the runner's high. Sex with a partner is physiologically more stimulating than sex with oneself, and sex with a *forbidden* partner is even more arousing. The dose of stimulation that arises from the combination of sex and fear is likely some of the underlying impetus and "pay off" in clergy/parishioner sexual abuse.

The crossing of taboo relationship barriers enhances the chemical arousal system, and the rush of feelings that accompany the encounter can be interpreted (or misinterpreted) as love. When we idolize those who break away from holiness and sexual purity and then romanticize their fall into sin, we set up dangerous relational mythologies.

Lust is often depicted as unholy desire. The act of bringing down a saint with seduction, the first encounter with a virgin, the desire of a holy man for things carnal—these themes have long been part of our culture's collective unconscious and have exacerbated the problem of sexual abuse in communities of faith.

Sex Is Situational

Sexual norms and behaviors in one situation may be different from sexual norms and behaviors in another situation. In one context, we describe "a great love affair" in glowing terms. In another context, we use the term *affair* with a full measure of heavy condemnation. What may appear to be sexually ethical for mature 50-year-olds may not be for 18-year-olds. While a member of a congregation may hold a bachelor party with a seminude dancer, a pastor would be expected to keep a different standard.

Other situational factors include differing cultural norms and expectations. Some congregations experience angst at the appointment of a divorced clergy person, and in some cultures divorce is still an act that shames the community. In other settings, such as a diverse urban church, a lesbian pastor and her partner are welcomed and celebrated.

When we acknowledge these situational factors, we allow for conversations rather than legalisms. We reduce the tendency to prescribe the "right" sexuality for everyone, and we open the way for dialogue. When we talk about the situations that enhance the holiness of sexuality and those that are damaging, we begin to name and therefore prevent abuse.

Prevention entails a good deal more than telling the offender what to do or not to do. It involves clergy and laity learning to make wise decisions, and to recognize high-risk situations. If there were a way to lay down laws for clergy behavior in every circumstance, then instruction might be effective. But the unique situations of each parish, and each pastor's changing needs and circumstances across his or her lifetime, make it impossible to do that.

> ***For Personal Reflection***
>
> What kinds of sexual situations might you label "holy," and what kinds might you label "destructive"? When have you engaged in high-risk sexual behavior? What contributed to that experience? What did you learn from it?

Congregations have often overlooked their role in creating an atmosphere for healthy communication about sexuality. Blame and shame approaches have tried to eradicate abuse by changing the behavior of individuals within the system while ignoring the system as a whole. Workshops for laity have suggested that congregations scrutinize the pastor's every move. We have, in effect, said, "The perpetrator is the problem." However, pointing to an individual as the only source of the problem has not helped reduce overall incidents of sexual abuse in congregations. Whether the abuse takes place between the pastor and staff, the pastor and a parishioner, staff and parishioner, or between parishioners, every person in the congregation is affected by it and may have subtly and unconsciously contributed to it. The removal of an isolated violator may be a first step, but does not in and of itself make the congregation safer. The ongoing relational needs of the congregation and the violator must be addressed. Intervention in the whole system is necessary. If the incident is shrouded in shame and secrecy, the problem is likely to occur again in the future.

A partnership is needed among laity and clergy in order to analyze the situation from both individual and congregational dynamics. What aspects of the congregation's life may have set the stage for sexual boundary violations? What can be done to create situations where safety is everyone's utmost concern? Congregations need to welcome truth speaking. To provide safety and to educate congregations about misconduct of a sexual nature, laity and clergy must both be free to discuss situations in which sexuality enhances and uplifts and those situations where risk and damage may occur.

Sex Is Complex

The first three guiding principles (that sex is powerful, relational, and situational) lead us to the fourth principle—that it is tremendously complex.

I've been leading clergy and laity workshops about creating safer congregations for over 10 years and find that the topic gets more and more complex. Every time I draw a line or state a rule about appropriate sexual behavior, someone in a workshop finds an exception, and we go back to the proverbial drawing board. I am the first to admit that no one answer is right in all situations. I look for underlying principles and values that can be agreed upon and then try to address each problem from principles rather than from rigid or legalistic formulas.

It's hard to allow for complexity *and* establish guidelines. It's especially hard for trained clergy to avoid preachy and didactic approaches! Every story in this book can be read and followed by a "what if" question. In live workshops, we use these "what ifs" and come to some consensus. We acknowledge that we cannot totally eliminate the risk of sex abuse by creating hard and fast rules. We do, however, develop processes and policies that acknowledge the complexity of human sexuality and reduce the risk of sexual abuse.

Through dialogue in your congregation you will be able to effectively apply this material. If, when interpreting this material to your congregation, you become legalistic, some individuals will find ways around what you have said. They may experience the message as blaming or shaming. People who engage in sexual abuse and sexual boundary violations find ways around rules, no matter how thorough you have been in establishing policies and procedures. You will not find material in this book that describes every situation and what to do about it. You will find instead guidance on beginning conversations about ethical sexual behavior. You will find ways to work within your congregation to address the powerful, relational, situational, and complex nature of human sexuality and sexual abuse.

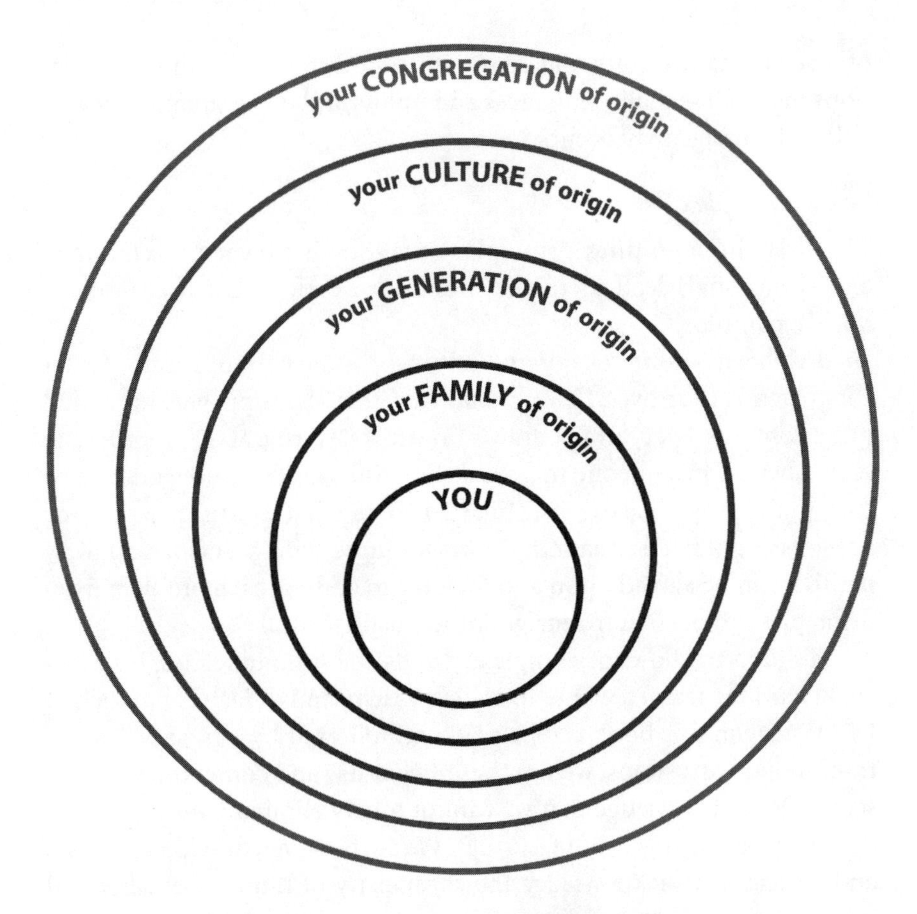

How You Learned about Sex

TWO

Family, Generation, Culture, Congregation

The Context

Every one of us has learned about sexual attitudes and behavior from a young age. In our families we learned when and how to touch others and ourselves. We learned that in one context, touching certain parts of the body is okay and in another context it is not. We learned how close to stand to someone and when and how to make eye contact. We learned to think of our bodies as good or as evil or some combination thereof. In the overlapping circles of family, generation, culture, and congregation we have learned nearly all that we now believe about sexual attitudes, attractions, and behaviors.

Your Family of Origin

How did you learn about sex? Perhaps you were raised on a farm or watched mating animals during a 4-H project. You may have been handed a book to read by a parent who was too embarrassed to talk with you about sex. Perhaps a buddy came along with some information. You may have learned about sex from an older sibling. Do you remember when you learned about sexual intercourse? I remember the exact day and time that I was told about it. I was walking home from junior high school, and some girlfriends gave me the full story in graphic detail. I remember being shocked and horrified.

Most of what they said was new to me. At school we'd watched films about menstruation and such, but no one had told me exactly how the sperm gets into the vagina. This was part of the lesson the teachers left out. They also left out the part about the woman's sexual arousal system.

A Sex-Ed Story

When my daughter was old enough for sex-ed at school, the teachers sent home a packet of information about the program. It included a curriculum outline and pictures that they would be showing the students. I was upset. I phoned the school nurse and said, "This is Reverend McClintock and I have a complaint about the curriculum." She thought that she'd run into a person who didn't believe in sexuality education in school.

"You can sign a waiver and your daughter doesn't have to participate in the class," she said quite politely.

"That's not the problem I'm having with it," I said. "The problem I'm having with it is that the clitoris is not on the picture."

"What?" she said as she knocked over her coffee.

"Well," I continued, "I can't see how it's fair that the boys get a lesson in arousal and that the girls don't." She apologized and noted that her goal was not to teach anything other than reproduction.

"Do you think the species would really continue if women didn't find sex somewhat personally rewarding?" I asked, and I begged her to update her pictures.

I ask participants in my workshops to explore their first encounters with information about sexuality, and I encourage you to trace your own sexual knowledge back to its roots. It helps us lighten up about the subject of sex. It also directs us to our own stories, where our beliefs and experiences are formed. Across all age groups and cultures, people seem genuinely surprised at how little information they were given about sex at school or home. Given this background, we tend to repeat the pattern and keep silence about all things sexual.

As you prepare to talk about sexuality in your congregation, review your own sex education. What were the messages about sex and gender in your family? Our family had a strong taboo against talking about sexual things, so as children we learned to feel embarrassed about it. We were strictly forbidden to talk about menstruation at the dinner table or anytime dad was around. My sister and I could only have boys over to the house if there were a bunch of girls there, too. (My parents ascribed to a "safety in bunches" theory.) When some neighborhood boys carved a sexual symbol in the snow in our front yard one winter, my father asked what it meant. My sister looked at me, blushing. I looked back at her, pleading. We both claimed ignorance. It's nearly impossible to talk about sex with your parents. To her credit, Mom had given us the "you can talk with me about anything" speech, but we knew that it would horrify her if we really did.

When there is shame about sexual desires, behaviors, abuse, or addiction in families, the system shuts itself down with what is commonly called a "no-talk" rule.[1] Most family systems have "no-talk" rules. The intent of the silence in a healthy family system is to protect the parental privacy. It establishes a boundary between the adults, who are sexually mature, and children, who are curious and exploratory, yet lack wisdom and judgment. The problem with the no-talk rule is that it also covers up sexual secrets about matters such as sexual abuse, adoption, affairs, homosexuality, pregnancies, and abortions. It eliminates conversations that are needed. The "no-talk" rule has kept many an incest victim from speaking the truth about what has happened to him or her.

> ***For Personal Reflection***
>
> How did you learn about sex? What aspect of the information was helpful? What was left out of the information you received? Did you receive information at age-appropriate times, or too early or too late? What were the no-talk rules in your family? What were the reasons behind the silence?

Your Family in Context

In some cultures the no-talk rules apply not only within the family but beyond the family. In the illustration on page 16 I have drawn four circles around the *You* in the center box, but in some cultures the center box would simply contain the word *family.* Individual actions are considered valuable or shame-producing depending on the effect they have on the entire family.

Family members protect themselves from feelings of shame about violations of sexual norms by silencing those who have been victimized. Stories of "shameful" behavior become family secrets. One or more members of the extended family may be designated to be the spokespersons for the family and responsible for the dissemination of information about things that are considered sexual deviations. This person protects the family by monitoring what information is shared both within and beyond the family. This silence, while seen as a protection for the family as a whole, limits the healing of individuals who have been sexually violated. Telling the story, and having others receive the story as true, are crucial stages in the healing of individual sexual shame. The reputation of the family as a whole may be saved by a silence that prolongs individual pain. These are decisions that each family makes when handling sexual issues.

You may know about some of your ancestors' family secrets. Each family has a few. They may be related to courtship, living together, pregnancies, affairs, or sexual orientations. Or they may be about sexual violations such as rape or incest. Each of these secrets is handled differently within the family. You have made decisions about which of them to tell, and which to keep quiet. You may be involved in a decision about that right now.

What you learned in your family about sex includes what you have been told or not told about these family secrets. You learned who you could talk to about what, for what purpose, and when. Some of the secrets you have chosen to keep and others you have talked about more freely.

For Personal Reflection

What are the sexual secrets in your family? How did you learn about them? How have these been handled? Who holds the power to decide which of them to tell and which of them to keep secret? Are there sexual secrets that you would like to be free to talk about in your family?

Your Generation of Origin

Your attitudes about sex were formed during your years in a specific family whose messages were passed down to you. You learned these things at a time in history that is unique to your generation. You rebelled against and discarded some of the former traditions of your family. Some of them you kept. If you are a parent, you will pass spoken and unspoken messages to your children about sex and sexual secrets.

Sexual norms and values in families don't stay the same from one generation to the next. Sexual issues such as age of first intercourse, marriage or cohabitation, and sexual orientation are changing rapidly across generations. Polls have shown that three-fourths of 20- to 30-year-old people support civil unions for gay men and lesbians, but only one-fifth of people over 60 feel that way. The definition of marriage is an explosive political and religious issue.

Over the past 30 years in the United States, we have seen a decline in the marriage rate, a rise in the divorce rate, and an increase in cohabitation, which some now estimate at nearly 50 percent of adult couples. The average age of first sexual encounter has dropped by several years into the preteens. Virginity at the time of marriage is no long the prized treasure it once was, and is in some circles considered odd.

One of the most dramatic changes in sexuality education experienced by today's younger generations is the availability of information about sex in the media. Sexuality education has moved to the television screen where programs include specific information such as the name and use of sex toys. This information is readily accessible on videotape as well as television. The media have also broadened cultural views about homosexual behavior. The rise of the Internet has fostered a new level of sexual awareness and information, while also marketing the use of a powerful behavioral addiction: computer pornography. The media have exposed sexual abuse in the military, the workplace, and congregations. These changes are confounding for everyone. No 30-year period in history has seen such rapid changes in sexual behavior or more public disclosure about subjects that were once strictly private.

While the media have moved to the forefront of sexual education, they have not felt compelled to present ethical conundrums, moral principles, or even the dangerous consequences of sex without emotional, spiritual, or literal protection. Generations of young people are unaware that sexuality is directly connected to the search for intimacy, and the longing for communion with the soul of another.

A friend of mine made me a T-shirt to wear at workshops that says, "Sexuality and Ethics" on the front in bold letters. I had no idea what wearing it in public would mean. After all, our culture is full of T-shirt logos, signs, designs, and messages. I came across some women's T-shirts in a small-town store that said "Eat Me" and "Porno Star." When I compared my shirt's slogan to those possibly dangerous messages, I expected little response to my T-shirt.

I wore it on a road trip to Reno, Nevada, where billboards advertise gambling and sex, thinking I'd be barely noticed. As I crossed the Sierra Mountains heading east into Nevada, I stopped in a little town at a Subway sandwich shop. There wasn't a customer in sight, just two 20-something young men cleaning the front windows. As I approached I saw one of them poke his elbow into the ribs of the other one and point at me. They were staring at the writing on my shirt.

They retreated to the other side of the counter as I entered, and I heard one of them say to the other, "I don't get it." And the other said back, "Well, I don't get it either." And herein lies the problem. Sexuality and ethics are two words rarely seen together in any venue: not in families, not in education, not in congregational life, not in the culture beyond the congregation.

People in their twenties have a very different view of sexuality from the 60-year-olds. The 20-year-olds were educated about sex by HBO television, where *Sex and the City* actors and actresses served as role models for those engaged in sexual exploration. The 60-year-olds, with fear and trepidation, learned about sex on their wedding nights.

Each generation likes to think of itself as more sexually liberated than the one before it. My father called my German grandmother "prudish." I use words aloud that my father would never have spoken in private. The pastor who preaches about sexual issues might receive rave reviews from some groups within the congregation and harsh criticism from others. While younger generations readily engage in discussions about sex with their peers, older generations have been taught that sex simply should not be discussed in polite company. When your congregation begins to discuss sexual behavior, what issues are likely to arise depending on the generation of the participants?

For Personal Reflection

How have the media affected your ideas about human sexuality? Have television programs been helpful to you in explaining issues to your children? Have you limited your exposure to certain programs and computer images? If so, why? If not, why not?

A Cross-Generational Experience

Cross-generational issues arose in one parish when a pastor disclosed to his congregation that he is gay. I was called in to serve as a consultant for them. My first task was to listen to the leadership team describe their congregation. Their stories helped me to become aware of the diverse generations and cultures within the congregation.

The congregation had three distinct peer groups, divided by age. I'll refer to them as the long-timers, mid-lifers, and young adults. When they were informed that their beloved pastor of seven years was gay, the age groups (with a few exceptions) responded differently. The long-timers had grown up in families and congregations that never talked about human sexuality. Sexual issues were seen as strictly private. The long-timers held to this value system as the issue erupted, and they were ill prepared to handle it, having no experience discussing any aspect of sexual behavior.

The mid-lifers were raised in the "question authority" generation. They were angry that their pastor had kept his sexual orientation a secret. They wanted to get the whole situation out in the open. What others saw as privacy, they saw as secrecy. The old-timers and the mid-lifers took opposite approaches to the whole situation.

The remaining group of young adults couldn't figure out why the church was wasting time on the pastor's sexual orientation when there were so many other needs in the community. They found the reactions of both the older groups to be overblown and, frankly, ridiculous.

During the consultation it was essential that various groups talk about the values and norms with which they were raised. We had to honor the diversity of thought among the members before we could begin to process new information about the pastor's sexual orientation. This involved education about the continuum of sexual orientations and the likely biological and psychosocial elements within one's orientation.

Early in the day a high-school boy in one of the small groups asked an older man, "Do you mean we're here because Pastor's gay? What's the big deal about that?" The man was honest and said, "Son, I'm not really sure." I later heard the man telling the group that he considered fidelity to be a more important concern for him than sexual orientation. With tears in his eyes, he reported that he had been faithful to his wife for the whole 54 years of their marriage. That teen learned a lot that day about value-centered sexuality. He heard an older man telling him about fidelity, a word that he'd never even heard before. The older man learned that his younger friend found it easy to affirm sexual difference. As they witnessed to each other and heard each other, both of them grew wiser and more compassionate.

At our afternoon break, I put bowls of Hershey's Kisses on the tables. I heard a man say to his wife, "I gave Harry some Kisses. Is that okay?" He was not being at all sarcastic, as a person of fear might have been. He was being playful. He was exploring the boundaries within his own generation alongside other generations.

We need each other when we dialogue about issues of human sexuality. Younger generations embolden the elders, and the elders are role models for the younger ones. In this situation it was marvelous to witness several generations engaging in heartfelt dialogue and personal growth while sharing their common commitment to the congregation as a whole.

Your Culture of Origin

Let's now look at the next circle on the graph from page 16: your culture of origin. You may be from more than one culture—most people are. A battle brewed over the recent census because there was no "other" category in which people could write in the many different branches of their lineage. Most people have one dominant cultural view of the world, and some less dominant cultures of influence. One definition of *culture* is a group of values, beliefs, attitudes and behaviors that are all shared by a group of people based on their ethnicity or racial group. The culture is defined by its rituals, social, educational, economic, and geographic variables. In each culture, sexual issues are handled quite differently.

In one culture young people are expected to marry before puberty; in another, to abstain from sex until early adulthood. In one culture sexual exploration through masturbation is expected; in others, forbidden. In one culture it's expected that young men and women go to prostitutes to learn about sex before finding marriage partners. In another culture, a man may marry several wives.

You may feel nervous about speaking to one another about sex, especially in a context of multiple cultures. Letting people tell their unique stories is a good place to start. You will learn about sexuality, gender, and racism and about the ways that these three overlap.

> *For Personal Reflection*
>
> Take a moment to think about sex and courtship within your culture. When and how do people initiate physical contact? What criteria determine dating and marriage rituals? When is sex appropriate or not and why?

Sexual prejudices have been used to shun or shame people within groups. One way people have used sexuality to reinforce racism is around issues of the amount and variety of sexual behavior in a given culture. Another way sexuality has joined with racism is about the sexual features of a person, the size of a person's lips, breasts, or penis. Hate crimes have been committed out of fear of the sexual power or activity that dominant cultures consider to be a deviation from the norm. None of us are completely immune to these prejudices. Your dialogue may help you and others to uncover the seeds of racism that lie within the topic of sexuality.

When I engage in cross-cultural dialogue about sexuality, I regularly remind myself, and I also remind you, that we are different. Jesus' mandate to "judge not" is certainly a must when discussing sexuality and culture. If a sexual behavior offends me, I have an obligation to explore my own discomfort about it before moving to judgment.

I am initially not so much interested in right or wrong as I am in seeing the world from another person's view and understanding it.

> *For Personal Reflection*
>
> In your culture, what are the sexual expectations of single people and married partners? Are there different expectations for male and female sexual behaviors? What are some stereotypes about sexuality within your culture?

One Model of Handling Sexual Issues

Sexual issues are handled quite differently in each culture. All cultures have ways to protect against damage to the family as a whole, and all of them have ways to deal with victims and perpetrators. One culture would put a perpetrator in the stocks in the public square. Another would stone a woman who violated a code of sexual behavior. We have learned of numerous ways that people who cross sexual boundaries are punished from movies, novels, and history books. We have less information about healing processes that actually work in dealing with sexual transgressions. One example that has been in good stead for many generations, however, comes from the Hawaiian culture.

In the Hawaiian culture, a sexual issue or problem in the family is brought to a meeting of the elders. The meeting, called the *Ho'oponopono*, is held when a transgression has taken place. It is designed to get the family together to assess the situation, discuss it, and provide means for repentance, restitution, and forgiveness. Prayer is an essential element in the process. Mary Kawena Pukui, an author with expertise in Hawaiian culture, describes the *Ho'oponopono*: "The idea . . . is to keep it in the family and have all the immediate family taking part." The meeting is a way to protect the family, and to take care of the issue and resolve it.[2]

I'm quite taken by the model of *Ho'oponopono* as an example of the way a family and perhaps a church family could handle a perceived breach of sexual ethics. A formal gathering of the elders could discuss sexual issues and seek to resolve them before the situation escalates. This process is more like mediation than litigation and resolves conflicts effectively. This is one example of the many processes we can learn from various traditions to help us discuss and resolve sexual boundary violations.

Your Congregation of Origin

I asked a group of 50 people what they learned about sex in their congregations of origin, and they just laughed. And then the room became silent. They were puzzled by the question. Someone eventually burst out, "Nothing!" There was laughter again, and with the laughter the air moved back into the room. And then I challenged them to go into small groups and talk about this. The room was soon bustling with energy. A woman remembered her Sunday school teacher telling the girls that Mary was a virgin and therefore they should be too. Another one remembered being told to cross her legs so that her shiny black shoes would not show her underwear. Another participant recalled a youth trip in which he learned a lot from his peers in conversations after lights out.

People in one group discussed sexuality from the wedding rituals they observed or participated in. A clergywoman noted, "The bride is passed over to the groom as if he'd bought and paid for her. The veil over her face is a symbol of the innocence that she was about to lose." A participant from a Christian community in Fiji told about the marriage ritual and days that followed. The couple's first sexual experience took place on the Sunday following the wedding. People gathered outside of the bride and groom's home and awaited the dawn to see the ritual cloth with the bloodstains on it, which proved the bride's virginity. The family was then rewarded for her virginity by the giving of gifts. As participants talked together around the tables, they found that they all had stories to tell about rituals that reflected the mores of their congregations.

One person described proper behavior for church life in America in the 1940s and '50s, when you weren't allowed to hold hands in church. A former Catholic man told of being hit with a ruler on the back of the neck by a nun he called Sister Mary Vicious for touching his girlfriend's hand during mass. Choir members mentioned the fact that even now they sit behind privacy panels (also called modesty rails). That way the congregation is free from the distraction of bare legs during worship. The pastor (presumed to be heterosexual and male) was saved from sexual distraction by the wooden barrier so that he could not see the legs of women in the front row.

A woman from an African Methodist Episcopal congregation recalled that the women of her parish used food as a kind of symbolic seduction. If you could get the pastor's or the elder's attention by baking the best pie, you were among the most honored and powerful women of the parish.

The Spoken Messages and the Silences

Workshop participants in small groups discovered that they, in fact, had learned a lot about sex at church. From very subtle attitudes and behaviors, they learned about gender roles, flirtation and seduction, sexual taboos, appropriate dating behavior, and sexual deviance.

Participants had learned about sexuality from experiences in their childhood congregation and in subsequent faith communities. Those congregations communicated about the boundaries and norms of sexual behavior through both words and behaviors, which were upheld with silence and secrets. They learned how dangerous sex can be. They learned to connect the word *sex* to the word *sin* and to connect sexual behavior to the feeling of shame. In one parish, an unmarried pregnant adolescent was brought to the steps of the altar and condemned by the pastor in front of the entire congregation. In another, the ushers escorted a young couple to the podium and forced them to confess their sexual activity "in the sight of God." When a synagogue had a baby shower for all of the new mothers, a mother who was single was not invited.

As participants in workshops reflected about what they learned about sex in their congregations, group leaders listed their ideas on write-on boards for everyone to see. These lists included warnings such as "don't talk about it," "it's bad," "don't do it," "only in marriage," and "masturbation will make you go blind." Sometimes a more hopeful note was added to the list up on the board: "God designed us that way" or "it is holy." These positive messages are in a small minority. And this is part of the problem.

For Personal Reflection

What did you learn about sex in your congregation(s)? Were you told about it, or did you learn these things in other ways? What were the unmentionable "sins" that you learned about? What have you learned about sex in your present congregation?

Indirect Messages

Most congregations have an underground communication system. When people tell me that everyone in the church knows about a sexual abuse in the past, I ask, "Everyone?" I was at a luncheon where Sue, a senior pastor, said to people around her at the table, "Everyone at my church knows that the former pastor crossed a sexual boundary." Her newly hired education staff member happened to be sitting across the table. He looked up, and said, "I didn't know that!"

A consistent theme from participants of my workshops is that much of what they learned about sex in church came from the rumors that floated around about it. Unexplored gossip can undermine the effectiveness of clergy or lay leaders, depending on whom the gossip is about. Gossip distracts congregations from matters of mission and service. I have experienced too many prayer chains that were actually the relay stations for a complex network of communications. The careful placement of a rumor about something sexual can disrupt a congregation for months. Conversely, the careful handling of rumors is a way to prevent small things from becoming big ones.

Healthy communication patterns can assist in risk prevention. When a situation arises regarding the pastor's behavior, what do people do about that? Questions taken directly to a pastor can be clarified and resolved. Sex abuse can be stopped in its tracks when parishioners have the nerve to directly approach the leader or clergy person and describe suspicious behaviors. Direct confrontation is difficult for most of us, but it can also reveal situations where there isn't anything wrong, as in the next example.

A Close Call

The following is a story of a rumor that could have exploded but didn't, due to the quick thinking and action of one congregation's member. One Saturday night, a couple in Pastor Frank's parish noticed Pastor Frank's truck parked at the adult video store in their community. The next morning after worship, Betty went to the coffee hour and whispered about it to others, who whispered to still others. Anxiety began to spread throughout the congregation. Before long everybody had heard about it.

If Betty had gone directly to the pastor after church and talked to him about what she had seen, the whole thing might have resolved itself. In this case, one of the parishioners who heard the rumor finally approached Betty and went with her to the pastor's office as everyone else was leaving for lunch. He said, "Ralph and Betty say that they saw your truck parked at the adult video store last night. Was that true?"

"Really," the pastor said. "I am so glad that you told me that. My son Rick borrowed the truck last night, so he and some college buddies could go out for a while. I'm so thankful that you told me about that. I'll speak to him." In just a few sentences a concern was resolved.

Rumors are just one type of unhealthy communication that can occur in a congregation. A congregation that has built open and direct communication patterns can prevent small issues, and even outright falsehoods, from becoming major problems. In such congregations, people reveal, examine, and think about the content of such a rumor before reacting to it. They speak up when they experience, witness, or hear about behavior that makes them feel uncomfortable. They speak directly to the person of concern without fear of embarrassment or retribution. Healthy communication handles suspicious situations effectively, without ignoring them or giving them undue credence.

You learned a good deal about sex from your congregation. Some of the information came from the things that people said, and some of it by what was not said. When you ask people in the church to talk to you about the congregation's history, ask them about secrets in the life of the congregation. Ask them about sexual affairs, boundary crossings, and other "indiscretions." You may come away quite surprised.

As you prepare to lead your congregation in prevention, take time to analyze current messages that are being sent to parishioners about sex. Do you know some secrets? Do others? Your careful consideration of the level of open discussion about sex that is going on right now will help you as you prepare to add more sexual education into the life of the congregation. Here are a few more questions.

For Personal Reflection

Do you talk about sex in your current congregation? What subjects related to sexuality and gender are included in scripture, teaching, exhortation, and prayer? Which ones can you talk about? Which ones are taboo? If you know about a rumor or a sexual secret in your congregation, will you risk revealing it? Why or why not?

Catalysts for Change

You have now reviewed your own family issues, the attitudes you may have from your generation, your cultural context, and the messages of your first congregation(s). That is a lot to consider before beginning a program on sexual abuse prevention. Do you feel ready to begin? Knowing your own background, your beliefs, your prejudices, and the no-talk rules that still come up in your thoughts and feelings today will help you engage with others in your congregation.

The word *prevention* means literally "to come before." In common usage it has come to mean something you do before something terrible happens. This isn't a book about what to do after something happens. It's about what to do before disaster strikes. I'm asking you to break the unhealthy family and congregational rule—the no-talk rule. Talk to your parents, the elders in the congregation, and to younger generations. Talk to people from different cultures. You will learn about yourself in the process.

You may have sexual injuries that need to be healed. You may have shame about a sexual experience that you have had. You may feel shame about a fantasy, a desire, or a sexual orientation. You may feel shame about being a victim or a perpetrator of abuse. That feeling of shame may have contributed to your silence, or perhaps you were told to keep a sexual secret. That shame will try to trick you into keeping silent yet today. And you may feel that you are breaking a taboo when you begin conversations in your congregation concerning sexuality. Breaking the no-talk rule is not as easy as it sounds on paper. It does get easier over time, and is worth the effort: by speaking the truth in love you can prevent sex abuse.

Your congregation needs people like you who have the courage to speak up. We have left the fascinating and challenging subject of sex out of congregational life for a few centuries too long. It is time to get everyone into the room talking about experiences, values, and morals. Complicated sexual issues may arise in the process of developing a plan for sexual abuse prevention. You may wish to consult a professional counselor about any of your own concerns that arise and about any group dynamics that you wonder how to handle.

On a recent Sunday I preached about the story of the incestuous rape of Tamar from 2 Kings 13. I had gone into the sanctuary that morning with fear and trembling because I had chosen such a difficult and uncomfortable text, but it was worth the effort. After the service was over, a gentleman and his wife approached me in the greeting area. He became overwhelmed with emotion as he said, "We need to talk about these things. It's the only way to change them."

I ask you to offer your congregation the gift of your courageous leadership. Below you will find a list of common fears about discussing sexual abuse. Place a checkmark by the sentences that pertain to you. Then review the list of motivations and place a checkmark by the sentences that pertain to you. Examine your fears, challenge them, and begin the dialogue. Break the no-talk rule and begin the process.

Common Fears about Discussing Sexual Abuse

- Fear of talking openly about any sexual issue
- Fear of offending others for whom the no-talk rules are inflexible
- Fear of exposing unhealed sexual issues, experiences, traumas, and pleasures
- Fear that we will bump into feelings of shame in others or ourselves
- Fear that we will invade someone's privacy
- Fear that we will say something stupid or embarrassing
- Fear that we will express or expose a judgmental attitude
- Fear that we will expose uncomfortable disagreements about the Bible and faith
- Fear that the congregation will be divided when differences are exposed

Motivation for the Prevention of Sex Abuse

- The readiness to act on the dream of safety and respect
- The desire to discuss sexuality and to understand diversity
- The desire to affirm your own sexuality as a gift of God
- The desire to be free of constricting or outdated ideas and ideologies
- Readiness to acknowledge past sexual secrets in the congregation
- Readiness to acknowledge failure, danger, and damage in the congregation
- The desire to speak the truth lovingly and respectfully
- The desire to be seen as the individual you are and to be blessed rather than rejected
- The desire to live free of shame, and in a state of grace toward yourself and others

THREE

Sexual Harassment

What It Is and What to Do about It

I was erasing the board when a student in one of my ethics courses shyly approached. I could see that he was upset, his face was flushed. We set an appointment for later that afternoon.

I was concerned as I awaited his arrival at my office. What could have triggered such a strong physical and emotional response? Was he the victim of harassment? Did he know someone who had been a victim or a perpetrator?

Throughout the semester he had been under a lot of pressure, ministering to a rural community church and commuting to school for a counseling credential. We are both ministers, yet our theological training was as different as night from day. He attended a small Baptist seminary in the early 1990s where there were no women among his teachers or his colleagues. I attended Pacific School of Religion in Berkeley during the 1970s. He is a first-generation South American immigrant, tall, and has a deep lovely voice. I am four generations away from my immigrant ancestors and the descendent of several clans of small Europeans with brogues. Although I was concerned about him, I also welcomed the learning that could come from our exploration of sex and gender.

He arrived promptly. We chatted about his congregation and the pleasures and challenges of serving there. This led him to his concern from class. He said, "I am not sure of the rules in this country, because what I have learned before is different." Rules about sex and gender are some of the more complex dynamics of every culture. His cultural upbringing and his theology clashed with the information I had presented in class. Could a woman file a charge against a man just for his comment about her beauty, or her dress? Was it wrong to hug someone without asking him or her first? Could he get in trouble for hugging the children at his parish? In his culture, it would be an offense *not* to hug the children.

He explained his role as pastor to me. "I want to know specifically what is right and what is wrong. It's my job to tell this to the congregation." Our class had not given him what he needed. To him the information lacked specificity.

Was I asking him to erase some of what ha had been taught from his personal hard drive? He had been taught that men and women are different and should be treated differently. Why is it that in harassment charges the recipient determines the offense of the action? He was raising good questions.

My ethics class presented him with new situations with different values and principles. In both his culture and his theology there are rules and there are punishments for breaking them. We discussed the limitations and advantages of rule-based authority. With sexual harassment the issue is less about hard-and-fast rules and more about what is called situational ethics. A decision about how and when to touch the people in the parish cannot be reduced to one set of rules. Every situation is different; every person is different.

His role as a teacher for his congregation was paramount to him. As is true for all clergy and laity, he would eventually be in a situation that required him to address issues of sexual behavior. This can be done proactively or reactively. Although his cultural way to deal with these issues is different than the way of the dominant U.S. culture, he is serving in a congregation where state and federal laws about harassment still apply. The fact that he was willingly addressing his own discomfort and talking about taboo subjects was a reflection of his moral strength. With his knowledge of both cultures he is uniquely able to help his congregation with these issues. I appreciated the way that he educated me that day and I celebrate that he has also led his people in the creation of a safe congregation.

Definition

Our discussion of sex abuse in the church begins with a look at one kind of sexual abuse known commonly as sexual harassment. Sexual harassment is defined as:

> Any unwanted sexual comment, advance or demand, either verbal or physical, that is reasonably perceived by the recipient as demeaning, intimidating, or coercive. Sexual harassment must be understood as an exploitation of a power relationship rather than as an exclusively sexual issue. Sexual harassment includes, but is not limited to, the creation of a hostile or abusive working environment resulting from discrimination on the basis of gender.[1]

Sexual harassment is complicated because there is leeway for interpretation within its very definition. You could say or do the very same thing to two different people and one of them would consider it harassment and the other one would not. A variety of behaviors may be considered problematic in one situation and just fine in another. The perception of injury lies with the victim. This leaves a lot of room for confusion, for cultural differences to be misinterpreted, and for litigation.

Definitions of harassment are established by personnel policies in congregations, denominational guidelines, and the law. Harassment may include something said, a touch that lingers, a hug unasked for, or too much information that is shared about a person's own sex life. It can include a premature or unwanted probing for intimate information about someone, making sexual comments or innuendoes about one's own or another person's body, showing someone a sexually graphic picture, or directing a person to Web sites with sexually explicit pictures.

The exchange of sexual favors for job advancement (*quid pro quo*—"this for that") is sexual harassment. It may involve behaviors that we also define as sexual abuse such as the invasion of the body by force, rape, sexual assault, incest, indecent exposure, statutory rape, or other forms of unwanted sexual behavior. Sexual harassment can also include a violation of someone's emotional self, such as the creation of an environment where people feel that they are treated in a biased way because of their gender or sexual orientation.

Once a recipient states that one of the behaviors described above is unwanted and undesirable, then the behavior must change or the individual and the organization (if there is one involved) could be liable. Each place of work, each congregation, has its own set of norms and practices about touch behaviors. Harassment charges are more likely to be filed if anyone within a congregation behaves in a way that is outside of those norms.

> *For Personal Reflection*
>
> What are the norms about touching in your congregation? How clear are these expectations to members and visitors? What happens when someone breaks one of these unspoken rules?

It's Not Always Touching to Be Touching

Schools, state agencies, and businesses have been training workers to know and understand sexual harassment for years. We have more recently started providing such training to congregations. People are learning to respect a level of boundaries in the workplace that is more restrictive than in their other environments.

Congregations have been slow to implement harassment policies, partially because they do not see themselves as workplaces. Congregations have more often identified themselves as families than workplaces. Those who feel they are part of a family when they are at church may have more lax attitudes about touching. We touch our families more than we touch coworkers in a business office. This family identity is used to justify a different sort of touch behavior. I hear people argue that families hug and touch each other. "We want our congregation to be warmer and friendlier," they say, as if "warm and friendly" was defined by the freedom to touch others without asking their permission.

Every person has a different level of comfort with touching and hugging, depending on family of origin, generation and culture of origin, and personal touch experiences. A newly assigned pastor was in a particularly difficult dilemma because of cultural norms and practices in her parish. On the day she arrived at the parish, she was told, "We're a hugging church." She was, therefore, expected to be a hugging pastor.

She also felt that if she hugged one person, she would have to hug them all. The pressure was on her, especially as she greeted folks heading out of the sanctuary after services.

She approached me at a break during one of my workshops. She disclosed her ambivalence about giving and receiving hugs. Some of the touches she received felt good to her; they felt genuine and safely casual. But some of the touches left her feeling uncomfortable. Some of them were too close, too intimate. One of the men gave her a full body hug she found uncomfortable, but she was not sure what to do about it.

In another job setting she might have had some kind of policy about sexual harassment to go by, but her church and denomination did not have one. She was on her own to set the standards and guide her congregation. She found the solution by increasing her awareness when she was in the receiving line after church. While she smiled and greeted people, she paid attention to her own cues about the touches that she was receiving. She began to actively choose whom to touch and how close to get to each person who came through the line. She could then redirect some of the inappropriate touches. She would extend her hand and keep her elbow locked to create a distance before she and the full-body hugger collided. She was relieved to find ways to protect her body from unwanted touch, and to touch different people differently.

With new choices available to her she was more lighthearted on Sunday. She discussed the issue of touches and hugs with others within the church. They discussed the spoken and unspoken rules that their church family followed. The congregation's initial resistance faded away, and the line "We're a hugging church" receded into the history books. The board replaced it with a new phrase everyone liked better. They decided to greet newcomers saying, "We're a caring community."

Boundaries to the Rescue

Setting a boundary about touch is a wise and respectful thing to do. Sexual harassment is unwanted and uninvited contact. Recipients of unwanted touch feel the powerlessness of being controlled by another person's behavior. A greeter approached me one morning outside of a local congregation where I would soon preach. He took my hand, held on tight, and then began stroking my arm over and over again as if I were a cat he was petting. I looked around, embarrassed by his behavior and unsure about how to stop it without a left hook to his jaw. I looked to see if anyone was watching. It is hard to project a professional image when someone is stroking your arm while talking to you. The whole thing was demeaning.

When people feel harassed, the environment does not feel safe. Unwanted touch and unwanted comments, looks, or *quid pro quo* (such as an exchange of sexual favors for job advancement) are disheartening, threatening, and extremely stress producing. The shame and embarrassment of these incidents is intense. A person who is harassed even one time feels powerless. When it happens repeatedly, self-esteem is damaged and the workplace or the worship place becomes a place of danger. When it continues, the person who is being harassed feels increasingly powerless to address the behavior. And in fact, in a setting that tolerates harassment, the person who objects to such behavior might experience repercussions, such as being discredited, denied professional or educational advancement, or threatened with job loss. Clergy who are sexually harassed may resign or be reassigned without explanation.

For Personal Reflection

Have you experienced sexual harassment? What kinds of unwanted touches or flirtatious comments have you been uncomfortable with? If you told anyone about those experiences, was it helpful? Was the situation resolved? If so, how?

Making Change Happen

Clergy and laity can effect change in the way that people touch each other, in worship, at prayer and healing services, in the office, and at social activities. Here are some steps that you can take to make your congregation a safer place for counseling, work, recreation, and worship.

1. Pay Attention to Your Intuitive Discomfort

No amount of training and no extensive list of rules can protect you as well as your own intuition can. The clergywoman in the story above was inclined, at first, to ignore her own intuitive discomfort. Since she did not know what to do and she felt confused about it, she chose to pretend that it was a small and trivial thing. The denial of your intuition can allow a problem to escalate with dire consequences.

A pastor told me that he felt uncomfortable with a woman parishioner's adoring comments to him, but that he ignored them. Before long it was clear that she took his silence as mutual attraction. In his office one day she crossed the room and kissed him before he even knew what happened. He stopped her behavior with a clear boundary. He told her that her kiss was unwelcome and unwanted. He told her that he was in a professional relationship to her as her pastor and that he was not interested in a romantic relationship with her. But since his words had been late in coming, the entire experience was extremely troubling and embarrassing for them both. If he had found a way to tell her earlier in the relationship that her flattery was uncomfortable for him and raised concerns for him, the situation could have been resolved more easily.

In families where children are being abused, the children are often told that they are overreacting or too sensitive. Go ahead and react, and go ahead and be sensitive. God has given you the abilities you need to be safe, as long as you pay attention to your emotional and intuitive cues.

2. Stay Tuned to Your Body

You need to keep your body and your brain working at the same time, which is not easy to do. Neurologists have proven that the pulse rate increases similarly in situations of fear and in situations of arousal, so it can be easy to confuse the two. Powerful emotional experiences temporarily disrupt cognitive ability. Did you ever hear someone say of a person newly in love, "He's gone nuts!" or, "She's out of her mind"? Well, it is actually true that people can become irrational in times of flirtation, attraction, taboo crossing, anxiety, and when experiencing both desired and feared touch.

When I heard that a married pastor had been found laying on the couch in his office with a woman who was not his wife, I was shocked. I wondered how in the world he could have thought that this was okay. When a church office volunteer walked in on them, he tried to dismiss the situation by saying that they were just taking a nap. I wondered what happened to that man's cognitive function, until I studied the very real mind-numbing effects of sexual attraction.

Recognizing that you are biologically hardwired to lose your brains for the purposes of mating, you still have to try to keep your wits about you. You can notice your own physiological responses and determine the source of them. Were you flirting, or was someone flirting with you? Were you looking at someone for a bit longer than usual? Was someone looking at you? If so, did your pulse rate increase? Catching these subtle changes in your own body can lead you to notice those distracting attractions.

3. Notice Who You Touch and Why You Touch Them

Safety begins with an awareness that others may be uncomfortable with your behavior if it seems particularly personal. Pay attention to your touch to see if you touch one gender more than the other, or one gender differently from the other. Do your hugs linger for a longer time with some people? If your touching and language toward both men and women is generally the same, no one could accuse you of having a gender bias in your behavior. You might not be accused of bias, but you still might be out of line—toward both genders. The only way to know when you are crossing someone's touch barriers is to stay awake and aware of your body, your feelings, your behaviors, and the behavioral responses of others. Pushing aside those little discomforts can lead to disastrous results.

> *For Personal Reflection*
>
> When is another person's touch uncomfortable for you? How do you touch women? How do you touch men? How do you touch children? How do you read the other person's comfort level?

4. Avoid Commenting on Appearance

A popular television ad shows a man who looks particularly good at work one day. Everyone asks what is different about him. Hair cut? New suit? In the ad it turns out that Joe looks so much better because he has taken Viagra. The implication of the ad is that he looks good because he is having sex or having better sex than ever. These comments about the man would be forbidden under some sexual harassment policies and guidelines.

In one real-life workplace, a coworker changed his casual look to a more formal one and wore a suit to the office. His female colleague said, "Mike, you look really good in that suit today." He beamed. Her boss approached her and said, "If you hadn't been part of this company for 20 years, I'd fire you today." She was told in no uncertain terms that she could not make any comments about a coworker's apparel or tell a coworker that he looked "good."

In my workshops, I throw out some complimentary comments about people's looks to see if they would be perceived as harassment. Depending on the tone of voice and inflection I use, participants' understanding of the words I say changes dramatically. Do I speak slowly? Do I lean forward as I speak? Do I pause? Do I smile? The very same words can be read as flirtatious, seductive, or complimentary depending on the culture and experience we each have, and depending on our gender roles and behaviors. Since the actual words can be misunderstood easily, workshop participants struggle to determine the best approach. Most participants end up concluding that comments about apparel, hairstyle, smell, or mood, are all in dangerous territory.

5. Ask Before You Hug

Asking is a simple guideline that really works. At first it may seem awkward, but later it becomes the norm. A video resource on sexual harassment called *Ask Before You Hug,*[2] distributed by the United Methodist Commission on the Status and Role of Women, provides scenarios for small-group discussion. One scenario shows a choir practice where a woman hugs everyone, even a man who is uncomfortable with it. It shows how he handles the situation firmly and with grace. Many other scenarios are offered. The video does not use professional actors, but the scenes do provide lots of food for thought. I recommend this film to you for use in your congregation.

I recently returned to a former parish to conduct a funeral service. The leaders had been to my training, had seen the video, and had gone back to their congregation and trained others. Each person who approached me said either, "Would you like a hug?" "May I give you a hug?" or "Could I have a hug?" In every case I hugged. I hugged one sideways. I hugged another briefly. I also knew that if I chose to, I could safely say, "No thanks, but I'm so glad to see you."

If the idea of turning down a hug is hard for you to imagine, try it a few times to see how it works. The harder it is to do, the more you will become aware of the pressure people feel when someone is crossing a physical or sexual boundary with them.

6. Ask Yourself, "Who Needs This Hug?"

Consider whether your touches are meeting your own needs or what you think the other person needs. Pastors have told me that they hug older single people more often than others because they feel that these older people need the hugs. While hugging has proven beneficial for mental and physical health, not all seniors—not even single seniors—are alike. Actually, there are some married people and some young people who never get hugs in their relationships. Assuming that another person needs your hug is dangerous. You need to double-check to see if your contact is really about your own need to be touched or your desire to feel closer to the person you touch.

7. Notice the Feedback

You can reduce the risk of being misunderstood by paying close attention to the verbal and nonverbal feedback you get from the people you touch. Do they respond in kind? Do they touch you back in the same way? Do they offer a limp handshake, or a quick pat? These signals can mean that the person may not want the touch. Some people will hug a pastor back just because he or she is in a position of leadership or authority. In some cultures a downcast gaze would mean that the person is ashamed of the level of contact that just transpired. In others it would be a sign of honoring the esteemed pastor. If in doubt, ask.

Once you have observed the physical feedback of others, modify your touch based on that feedback. If you match the other person's physical style, you can be relatively sure that you have behaved appropriately. If the other person stands a certain distance away, do the same: do not move closer. If the other person's hug is brief, do not grab on and linger. If the other person turns sideways, it may mean that next time you should offer a handshake.

8. Take the Risk of Being Called a Cold Fish

If you want to reduce your risk of being accused of sexual misconduct, simply reduce the amount of touching that you engage in. If you are a pastor who limits your touch in the church, you could run the risk of being thought of as cold and uncaring. Remember that you grew up with a certain level of "huggy-ness" that not everyone else grew up with.

In a cross-cultural ministry where the pastor and parishioners are from different cultures, the pastor needs to fully understand the touch boundaries of his or her parishioners. The parish could interpret a pastor's actions as a cultural offense. If you are clergy in a diverse congregation, ask leaders in each cultural group to assist you in knowing the distance to stand from others, where to look when talking, and touch behaviors. And then, like the young pastor in the introduction to this chapter, explain the reasons for your own touch boundaries by explaining the sexual harassment norms and laws in your state. Be intentional about your conduct and explain it fully to the personnel committee and the congregation.

> *For Personal Reflection*
>
> Under what circumstances do people in your culture hug or kiss? What kind of physical contact in public would be accepted in your culture between colleagues, friends, or lovers? When are you comfortable and when are you uncomfortable with public displays of affection?

9. Learn and Practice Safer Alternatives

Gender studies have shown that American women are acculturated to give lots of empathic head nods and verbal comments like "uh huh," and they do these things more frequently than men in a conversation. Men can learn this skill in order to be perceived by women as more empathetic, thereby foregoing the need to touch. Women have been taught to use words in expression of empathic concern more freely. Men have been taught to show their love through sexual intimacy and physical contact. There are safer alternatives for both genders, such as changing body posture, nodding the head, leaning forward, or using a simple phrase such as, "I can understand how you would feel that way."

I have learned to pay attention to my instinctual touch behaviors and allow space for those who feel vulnerable to touch. I carefully watch the distance that a person keeps in relation to me. I know that I can offer empathy through my tone of voice, the words I select, and even the careful placement of the chairs in the office. A client who had made good progress in therapy was at the end of her sessions. I asked her, "Is there anything you would like to say to me about how it's been for you?" Her response: "Thank you for not touching me." And she added, "All of my other counselors have touched me without even asking if that would be right for me." For this woman, the gift of restorative relationship depended on her feelings of utter safety with me. That included my full respect for her boundaries. She learned that I cared for her in other ways.

I was taught as a child to hug or touch people who were crying. It was part of our family and culture. And when someone in my office cries, I still want to do that. But I have learned not to touch so that my actions will never be misunderstood, and so that the one in pain will have all the space he or she needs to process the pain without my interference. I make sure that tissues are next to the person talking, so that I do not disrupt the flow of things. Even handing a tissue to someone can be distracting.

In the pastor's office, at a board meeting, or sometimes in the hallway at the church, people may cry. When that happens, the safest alternative is to stay nearby and to keep an open posture so that the individual can, if desired, lean into you, or ask for your embrace verbally or with outstretched arms. The embrace can be given briefly, and should never extend beyond the release of the one who initiated it.

10. Practice Ways to Express Concern

If you are a pastor, a parish nurse, a Stephen Minister, or other care provider in the congregation, here are a few options for you at the moment of another's expression of sadness or pain.

You can move your chair a bit closer. You can lean forward slightly. When a person is extremely sad, you can ask if he or she would like you to come and sit alongside of him or her in your separate chair. This conveys your presence and your care without ever touching. You can keep pillows and stuffed animals in the room as well, and offer them as comforts during times of pain. And lastly, when someone asks you for a hug, carefully consider what feels right for you as well as what the person needs. If you feel you can safely give the hug, go ahead. If not, say something such as, "I don't feel like that is best right now," and then offer to stay present, sit a while, listen, or pray.

I encourage you to think through these issues ahead of time. Without destroying the experience, you can become quite conscious of who you are touching, the context, the nature of the touch, and the motivation behind it. And you can adapt your touch behaviors when you are conscious of them.

> ***For Personal Reflection***
>
> What might you say if someone wants a hug and you are not comfortable giving it? What might you say if you feel like hugging someone and you are not sure how they would feel about it? What might you do the next time someone cries in your presence?

11. Avoid Gender-Directed Touch Behavior

One category of sexual harassment is gender-directed behavior. This could include jokes about one gender such as “dumb blond” jokes. It could include a tolerance for verbal comments toward one gender or the other. It could include the denial of advancement based on a person’s gender. When a woman colleague was denied raises by her parish for several years in a row, she was told it was because she had a husband to support her and did not need them. This was definitely discrimination based on her gender, and therefore sexual harassment. Gender-directed behavior can also involve different touch behaviors based on gender. It could include a pastor touching only the women of the church and not the men, or the women a good deal more than the men, or the women differently from the men. Different behavior toward either gender by either gender could be considered sexual harassment.

In the 2003 election of Gene Robinson to the Office of Bishop in the Episcopal Church, an issue arose about his touching a man in one of his previous congregations. After worship one Sunday, the priest briefly touched the upper arem of a man from his parish. The man was uncomfortable about it, but it was determined that the priest touched other people in similar ways and that this touch was not sexual or gender directed. The language of most ethics codes states that sexual harassment is “sufficiently severe or intense to be abusive to a reasonable person in the context.”[3] This is not to say that small discomforts should be overlooked. Any time someone perceives that a behavior is gender-biased or seductive in nature, the congregation needs to address the issue right away.

For Further Reflection: Two Case Studies

One way to learn about sexual harassment is to discuss case studies, either real or fictitious. Here are two situations for you to explore. As you review them, consider whether or not the incidents described constitute sexual harassment. They are both true stories that occurred in congregations. At the end of each scenario is a series of questions you might ask about these incidents.

Case Study 1: The Usher

I was on tour in an unfamiliar community last summer. I was staying with a couple I have known since seminary, and the three of us decided to try out a nearby congregation on Sunday morning. I was the first to step inside the foyer of the church, with Marta and Rudy behind me.

The elderly gentleman in the doorway reached out for me with both arms and surrounded my body with a bear hug. I stepped back (preferring not to hug a stranger that day) and took his right hand in mine. He said, awkwardly, "We hug everybody here." I told him that I would prefer a handshake. He turned to the little table behind him and passed me a bulletin. My friend Marta saw him coming and more quickly redirected his arms to a handshake, saying a polite "good morning." He passed her a bulletin. The third person in line was my friend Rudy, who is a gentle giant of a man, a kindergarten teacher at the neighborhood school. Rudy saw all of the activity in front of him and thought to himself, "I'd like a hug this morning." Moving with the flow of traffic in the entryway he stepped forward toward the man with an open and receptive posture. The man turned without even a handshake, picked up a bulletin, and using both of his hands for the pass-off, thrust it at Rudy and stepped back a little.

Was the usher conveying the sexual practices of his generation? Did he grow up learning that hugging women, even strangers, was acceptable, and hugging men—any men—was not? What else might the usher have been thinking and feeling?

Was the greeter's behavior gender directed? You could argue that it was not—that the usher responded to our corrections and kept a better boundary with Rudy. You could argue that it was gender directed, because the women were approached and offered hugs and the man was not even extended a handshake. Careful observation of his behavior

> *For Personal Reflection*
>
> What is your initial reaction to this scene? Why didn't the man hug Rudy? Was the touch behavior unwelcomed and unwanted? Would a reasonable person in this context view this as gender bias? If the man repeatedly hugged women and not men, would this be a problem? Is this sexual harassment? How did the behavior make the participants feel? What might you have done if you had been the pastor and observed this situation?

would be needed to determine whether the hugs were gender directed. One incident might not be problematic. But, if redirecting his behavior didn't stick and he continued to offer full body hugs to female visitors in the entryway, his behavior could be determined to be gender-directed behavior and sexual harassment. Was anyone else in the congregation uncomfortable with his hugging?

His pastor was a friend of mine, and she carried the story back to the ushers group for their discussion and consideration. The man was open to her feedback, and they all laughed a lot in the discussion. At first the ushers felt that it was a little silly for them to have to be aware of things like this, but in the end they appreciated the discussion. Some of them had been avoiding the job of greeter because they did not want to have to hug everyone who came in the door. With new permission and awareness, the number of people in the greeter pool increased. And the church is now safer for it. When everyone is offered the same physical greeting, a nod or a handshake, no one could accuse anyone of gender-directed behavior.

Case Number 2: The Joke

Lucy was assigned to a midsize suburban parish as its first female senior pastor. On the night of the annual meeting just a few months after she had arrived, the lay leader's welcome speech began with the following joke.

> "Did you hear the one about the clergywoman and the fishing trip? Well, there was a new woman pastor in town and she had to prove herself, see. So when a couple of the old cronies asked her if she could

go fishing with them, she said yes. They packed up their gear and headed out to the middle of the lake.

Once they stopped at the best fishing spot, one of those guys says, "I left the bait I need in my tackle box on the dock, but darned, I don't want to go back for it." The woman pastor, trying to be helpful, said she could get it. She stood up in the boat and walked across the water to the dock, got the bait, and walked back.

Those old guys were pretty impressed. They fished throughout the day, and she caught a lot of fish. That impressed them. But the next day she overheard them talking outside of Smithy's store. They were telling Smithy about her. They said, "Well, she can sure fish, but it's a darned shame she can't swim."

For Personal Reflection

If you were the new pastor, Lucy, how might you feel when hearing this joke? Is this joke gender biased? Does it reinforces or mock stereotypes about women? Would the joke feel different depending on the vocal tone and facial expressions used in presenting it? Does it add to Lucy's creditability as pastor of the church? If you were Lucy, how would you respond to this joke? Is this sexual harassment?

In your reflection, you may have considered that the story does have a stereotype within it, that women have to prove themselves to be accepted as equals with men. Another way to look at it is that the man who presented the joke was confessing the congregation's resistance to a new woman pastor and that he was trying to make a point of saying that they would overcome it with humor and grace.

A key way to consider the impact of a joke like this is to check in with the recipient of the joke to see if it felt like humor or sarcasm. Remember that harassment is behavior that is deemed by the recipient to be demeaning, intimidating, or coercive.

As the recipient of the joke, Lucy felt that the man's intention was to place her on notice, as if he were saying, "Watch out! We're not too sure we want you here. You'll have to prove yourself." Lucy remembered the joke many years later because it was attached to feelings of intimidation and disrespect.

The effect of the joke on Lucy is as significant as the joke itself. For her, it reinforced the cultural prejudice toward women who work in careers typically held by men. Social scientists describe the way that oppressed people internalize their own oppression. In college, Lucy's classmates had followed her into the bathroom with their Bibles to show her the passages that they interpreted to mean that women shouldn't become pastors. They told her that they considered her choice of vocation to be misguided and sinful. Hearing the joke triggered these old memories of humiliation.

The joke on its own might not seem like harassment, but given the repeated comments about women ministers that Lucy had endured over the years, she had internalized religious and cultural prejudices about her vocation.

This example describes what can happen when a person in a workplace has a history of being discredited and finds himself or herself in a similar (if not equal) discrediting environment. Lucy's decision about whether this was harassment or not would partially be based on her prior experience. The joke was not perceived by her to be neutral or supportive and it disrupted her ability to do her work. Lucy considered it to be harassment.

A Brief Review

Sexual harassment is a form of sex abuse, and if permitted, it can lead to even more damaging touch violations. Stopping a hug that is unwanted and honoring distance between two people is respectful and loving. If someone tells a joke that is possibly offensive or makes a verbal comment about someone's appearance, sexuality, or gender, do you speak up?

Most of us are not experienced in saying no to unwanted comments or touch. We want to be polite, and we have learned not to hurt anyone's feelings by being too direct or confrontational. And so we are too often silent.

Congregations have the opportunity to address the issue of sexual harassment through education. In the next few chapters, you will be learning what your congregation can do to reduce or eliminate sexual harassment through the development of effective processes and policies.

FOUR

Educating Your Congregation

We sometimes tolerate unwanted touch in congregations. For example, a high-school student in our congregation was recruited to organize games for a vacation Bible school program. When I saw him at church after the end of the first week, I asked how it was going. He said that the only problem he was having was that so many little kids were "jumping on me, slapping me, and clinging to me all the time."

"Why do you let them do it, if it bothers you?" I asked. He laughed. "I thought it was my job to help them discharge their energy on me." I laughed too, and said, "I thought they were supposed to discharge their energy running on the field, and with the ball. You can choose to be their punching bag or not, but I have an idea." I explained, "If you tell them that you want them to ask you before they slap you or jump on you, you'll be doing them a big favor, because maybe at home one of them is getting slapped and can't even find the words to say he doesn't like it. This is a good time to teach them the difference between recreational contact and crossing uninvited into someone else's physical space." He hadn't thought of it that way before and went back for another week, ready to defend his body and to help those kids learn that they too can set personal boundaries.

Where Do We Begin?

I suggest that you find out what your congregation currently knows about sexual boundaries, harassment, and abuse. Have members ever talked about sexual boundaries in program areas or worship? Do they know that without two people in a classroom it would be a dangerous idea to hug a child? Do your Sunday school children know about good touch and bad touch? Do you tell them how important it is for them to tell other people if they do not want to be touched, or did not like the way they were touched? Are youth in your youth program allowed to use sexual innuendo, jokes, or comments about physical appearance that might degrade or demean others? Do your adult programs include any curriculum about intimacy in marriage, or sexuality issues for adults both single and married? Does the curriculum you select include or avoid the subject of touch and sexual intimacy?

Here are some additional questions. Is the touch behavior your teachers use in classrooms, worship, fellowship, and meetings appropriate to the reasonable person in these contexts? Do ushers and greeters use various styles of contact, honoring customary boundaries for people of different ethnic backgrounds? Have you stopped to observe people giving and receiving touch? Do you as pastor, or laity, feel obliged to touch and hug as part of your leadership role? Do people sometimes say no to unwanted hugs or other touch? Have you noticed any touch behavior that is gender directed? These questions (and others that you will generate on your own) will guide you in establishing a program of education that spreads into every area of congregational life.

Educating Children

Unlike public school teachers, many church volunteers are not familiar with guidelines about physical contact with children. They need training to understand how to touch children safely in the classroom setting. Many congregations invite school professionals, childcare providers, and child protective services staff to provide in-service education for paid staff and volunteers who work with children.

A rule of thumb is to observe the child's body posture. If the child reaches out for a hug, ask him or her to use words and ask for a hug before moving into it. I watched a child therapist greet a little girl who was in treatment for abuse. She scrunched low to the floor and asked as the girl ran toward her, "Would it be okay if I gave you a hug today?" This question gave the little girl power to set her own boundaries. The little girl wanted the hug that day, but if some other day she did not, she would know that she could behave differently. Children may not feel they have the power to say no to someone's hug, so teaching them to use words is helpful.

Our congregations can become familiar with and utilize curricula that has been working well in local schools. About a decade ago public school systems began providing young children with education about good touch and bad touch. These programs help kids to deal with the fact that they might be approached in a way that makes them feel uncomfortable. They give kids knowledge about what to do if they are touched in private places. If your congregation has not yet included this type of education in the curriculum, that is the place to start. You can enlist the help of a local Head Start staff person or a schoolteacher.

What education are you providing for your Sunday school or religious school teachers? The first education to offer your volunteers happens in the recruitment and screening process. To ensure the safety of children, I recommend that volunteers who work with children and youth be screened when they are hired. An application and interview are not enough. While various state and county law enforcement agencies use different methods of running background checks, congregations can nearly always use these resources. In some areas, volunteers can be fingerprinted; in other areas, a local law enforcement agency will run a background check on staff and volunteers. Clergy can be role models for this process by going in and having themselves checked to learn about the costs and procedures. Volunteers in schools routinely go through this process, and though it may seem odd at first, understanding and supporting the reason behind the request will go a long way to show your volunteers that you are serious about protecting children.

Another guideline is that every classroom must have a window or doorway so that every corner of the room can be viewed from the hallway. Teachers need to be in pairs, and they need to be two unrelated adults. The reason for them to be unrelated is that in situations of sexual abuse, a nonparticipating spouse will sometimes cover up the problem out of loyalty to the spouse, the marriage, or a financial and emotional need to keep the family intact. In many situations of abuse, a silent witness is present.

To learn more about these dynamics and to further educate your staff about child abuse, congregations call upon local resources. Most state or county offices of child protection will come to your congregation and provide training about the signs and symptoms of abuse. When this training is embedded in the curriculum for children and adults, risk is greatly reduced. Adults who might have predatory intentions will discover that in your congregation any suspicious behavior will be named and stopped by the adults and by the children.

Education for children about touch boundaries needs to be imbedded in education programs for every age group. When we all learn to respect physical boundaries and to communicate our discomfort about touches, comments, or behaviors that distress us, we will create communities that are free of sexual abuse. For a complete list of guidelines for ways to protect children in church school, I recommend *Safe Sanctuaries* by Joy Thornburg Melton.[1] She spells out more specific ways to decrease the possibility that your children and adolescents would be abused in a classroom setting.

> ***For Personal Reflection***
>
> List some things that you could teach children to say to an adult who is touching them when they do not want to be touched. List some things that you could say to a child who is touching you in a way that is uncomfortable for you.

Why Worry about Touch?

A workshop participant approached me at lunch and asked, "Why all this emphasis on hugs and touch when we're trying to prevent abuse?" You may have thought of this question too. Yet sexual abuse all boils down to unwanted touch. It often begins with a hug and continues to a kiss and then to the touching of genitals. At the first sign of discomfort, at the first crossed boundary, unwanted touch can be stopped. It takes a level of assertiveness that few of us are taught as children.

Instead, many of us were taught to ignore our own intuition, and to let others cross our personal and physical boundaries. My mother always took me to the same shoe store to buy my shoes. The clerk was a loud, large, and authoritative older gentleman. His way of getting us kids to relax was to squeeze the tops of our knees with his thumb and forefinger. I protested. He thought that was part of the game, and so did my mother. If I got up to avoid him, they would tell me to sit back down. When I did, he would sneak another grab onto my tiny knee. As I write this paragraph, I can feel the anger rising up in my chest. In my body I can feel adrenaline rushing around seeking escape. At this very moment I want to knock him over the head with my little black patent leather Mary Jane's! I grew to hate shoe shopping. I would wear my shoes till they had holes in them. I would plead with my mom to find a different store to go to. She never got the message. I never directly told her what was wrong. Mother had repeatedly told me to respect your elders. I had no way to defend myself from this older man with a touch problem.

People of different ages cross people's touch boundaries. Some of them are teaching in the church school. Maybe the shoe store man teaches kids on Sunday mornings and does the same thing to them. Maybe the church people just say of him, "Oh, he's well intentioned"—again teaching the children to ignore their intuition or discomfort. When adults see children obviously squirming to get away from an unwanted hug or kiss, this is a teachable moment. But rather than talk to the child or the adult about this unwanted touch, most of us keep silent. We tacitly support this violation of a child's space.

Children who are abused in their families of origin are also told that they have to touch the adults or let the adults touch them, whether they like it or not. "Go sit on Uncle Ralph's lap, dear" seems innocent enough, but when the parents are away, Uncle Ralph's lap may not be a safe place. Many times, children try to talk about these things but do not have the words, or think that the adults do not care or will not listen to them. In their powerlessness, they go ahead and sit on Uncle Ralph's lap and in essence learn that they do not have many choices about touch. Without intervention, abused children grow up to be adults who allow their bodies to be violated and are at higher risk for becoming violators of others.

One of the reasons we teach children to ignore their own intuitions, preferences, and discomfort about touch is that we tend to wrongly assume that children always want to get hugged or that they need hugs from strangers. While they do, indeed, need safe touch (as we all do), these touches need to be based on the length of time the child has known you, the trust that the child feels in you, and the physical body language of the child in reaching toward you.

The little boy across the street has been dropping by my house for some time now. At first he kept a safe distance, as did I. So I was surprised when the other day in the driveway, I got out of my car and he came running toward me. I crouched down to be at his eye level, and he ran into me with his arms flung wide. I followed with a brief hug. How did I know how long to hug him? He told me with his body. After a brief second, he started wiggling, and I let go. Touch needs to be appropriate to the relationship. I'm available to him, but I let him define the touching. I do not pin him down, I rarely tickle him (and only after he starts the tickling behavior), and I do not allow him to hit his brother or me. In these simple ways, I teach him that both of our bodies are to be respected at all times.

When evaluating the touch behaviors at church, we have to consider the kids' perspective. Are they told to hug older people who make them uncomfortable? Are they told that they will disrespect the pastor if they do not do what he or she says, even if it is hugging or kissing? That kind of education only fosters children's feelings that they must obey older adults, even those who make them physically uncomfortable. That kind of education fosters sexual abuse, because it encourages children to be silent and compliant under the guise of obedience.

> *For Personal Reflection*
>
> As a child, when were you touched, hugged, or kissed in ways that were uncomfortable for you? What would you have wanted the adults around you to do? What would you like to have said or done to stop the unwanted behavior? What would you say or do now?

Encouraging Children to Say No and to Tell

Listen to the children. If every child in every Sunday school class were encouraged to say no to unwanted touch, there would be an immediate reduction in abuse. When the church mother says to her kids, "Hug the pastor, Dear," the pastor immediately needs to say to the child, "Only if you're sure you want to. It's okay not to hug me, too."

None of us is particularly good at turning down unwanted touch. And those who have not healed from physical, sexual, and emotional abuse grow up to be adults who are even less likely to speak up about unwanted touch. When you intervene and teach the children to turn down touch they do not like, you are well on the way to stopping abuse in the church or synagogue and in families and communities. Talking about these things in your education classes will stop the transmission of sexual abuse from one generation to another.

Children also need to be assured that if they tell someone about unwanted touch or abuse, they will be treated with respect and their story will be taken seriously. Once the children of the congregation know they can tell trusting adults about unwanted touch, incidents of abuse are reduced. These same children may also tell adults about abuse they are suffering at home. Teachers in education programs need to be trained to handle such reports through the superintendent, pastor, or directly with the child protective service office in each local community. When a child discloses abuse or neglect, professional staff (and some volunteers) are legally mandated to file a report with law enforcement or child protective services. More will be said of this in chapter 10.

For Personal Reflection

What is the phone number of the child protective services office nearest you? When do you think it would be possible to schedule a person to train the teachers in your children's program? Have the professional staff and directors of education programs for children and youth been fingerprinted? If not, why not?

Educating Youth

Can you recall a time in your teen years when someone made a hurtful comment about your body? Adolescents go through a development stage in which the look of the body becomes a central focus. Spurred on by the media and the ever-lowering age of first sexual exploration, teens spend a good deal of time and emotional energy on the issue of physical attractiveness. Teens no longer have to get their information from magazines in brown wrappers, however. They are able to buy them in the grocery store. An issue of *Cosmopolitan* can inform them about selecting and dating a sexual partner and about techniques to make their sex lives sizzle. Mainstream teens are being told to say no to everything except sex at a stage when they can think of little else. What is your congregation doing about sexuality education for youth?

Youth need lots of opportunities to talk about sex, yet most youth leaders are ill prepared to handle these issues. When I arrived at a congregation I was told that the youth pastor (a single male college student in his early twenties who was part-time on the staff) held meetings in which, the teens said, "We just sit around and BS about sex." He wasn't using any curriculum and no parents or volunteers were at the meetings, so anything at all could have been said. This situation put the youth participants at risk of sexual harassment or abuse, and even if the discussions were innocent, the congregation was in peril. Any teen participant could have said that the conversation made him or her uncomfortable and the church would have faced harassment charges. Correcting this situation became my top priority. I made sure a second adult was present at every meeting, I gathered more information about the discussions. I interviewed youth about the meetings to be sure that sex abuse had not taken place.

I honored the need of the youth to discuss sexuality issues by ordering new curriculum and bringing in two adults, one of whom was a licensed social worker, to teach it. While talking about sexuality issues can be a positive and preventative step, when it is a group consisting of one adult and a group of teens, it is definitely not advised. This was a high-risk program that luckily did not get out of hand.

Adolescents and Sexual Comments

A word needs to be said about the way that media culture permits rude and disrespectful comments about sexuality, sexual orientation, and parts of the body. While slanderous comments toward minority students have generally been stopped in private and public schools, sexual comments have been allowed to run amuck under the theory that these are harmless adolescent behaviors. Whether they occur at school or in youth ministries, these are far from harmless behaviors, however. Demeaning comments go to the heart of adolescent self-esteem and can become bullying and stigmatizing. When working with adolescents, particular care must be taken to stop gender-directed comments or comments about others' bodies. Careful curriculum development and trained facilitators will help youth to talk safely about sexuality.

Listen to the language that youth are using with one another, and then be prepared to stop inappropriate comments. The day that a young man called his brother a faggot, he was surprised that his youth leader took him into the office and told him that this term is unacceptable. It is a derogatory word that demeans homosexual people by comparing them to the wasted end of a cigarette butt, the faggot. Using it has the same damaging impact as using a racially prejudiced term. If teenagers are allowed to use harassing comments about gender, sexual orientation, or physical appearance, they are being allowed to harm others. To let this comment pass without correction would have taught the young man that he could disrespect others. Sexual harassment policies and guidelines do not exclude youth. If youth leaders let disrespectful and damaging language and behavior continue, the church is at risk for a sexual harassment lawsuit. It has to be named and stopped.

Many denominations are developing lesson plans to help teachers and pastoral leaders talk to teens about sex. Discussion in the curricula about values such as fidelity, respect, protection, and responsibility for consequences makes sexuality education at church distinctly different from what kids learn at school. Joy Thornburg Melton has also written a book called *Safe Sanctuaries* for youth ministry programs in which you can find additional ideas.[2] Issues of sexual harassment and abuse, as well as subjects such as sexually transmitted diseases and date rape, need to be addressed in a congregation's education program for teens every year.

> ***For Personal Reflection***
>
> What is your congregation doing to educate children and teens about sexual issues and values? How has your congregation responded to curriculum about sexual issues when it has been proposed? What is the content of the education in your public school system for adolescents, and how could you supplement that education in your church or synagogue?

Educating the Worshiping Congregation

Because the majority of people in the congregation regularly attend worship, this is an excellent place to begin the education process. Children, adolescents, and adults all gather on Sunday morning in worship. Clergy and lay leaders can teach consistent guidance about touch in the worship hour. When the subject is approached with a calm and even humorous tone, behaviors can begin to change. Many reasons for touch education, and many illustrations of how to do it, are included as you read the next few paragraphs.

Vulnerable Adults

One of the primary reasons we need to think about touch and sexual behavior in the context of worship is that many people who worship in our congregations on Sunday mornings have been sexually abused. One in three women has been sexually abused by the time she reaches adulthood, and one in ten men has been abused (though this figure could be low due to a reluctance to report abuse). Individuals who have been wounded by touch bring those fears and wounds with them to church in various degrees. On any given Sunday, however, neither ushers nor the pastor are likely to know which visitors or members have been sexually wounded. Body posture alone is not the key to determining this due to the many family and cultural variations on touch behaviors to begin with. Church members, especially ushers and greeters, can learn to pay careful attention to the physical actions of those they greet. We all need to be alert to the cues that others give us about what is comfortable for them. Here are some thoughts you might have in observing a new visitor.

Why is the new man on Sunday sitting by himself in the corner of the room? He needs to get to know us slowly; he's keeping a safe distance. We won't approach him right away. We'll give him the dignity of the space he has asked for. We won't just ignore him, though. In case he's wishing desperately that someone would reach out to him, we'll be sure to smile and say a word of welcome.

Our willingness and desire to be touched depends on the people involved, and various life circumstances. Touch needs change at different times. A widow who came to one parish recently told her pastor to stop hugging her for the first few months after her husband's death, because the feel of a hug from a large strong man reminded her of how it felt in her husband's arms. The feeling left her aware of how much she missed her husband's touch. She found that it was too much for her and she disintegrated into tears when he hugged her. She never told him why she needed a safer distance, but he sensitively complied with her request.

A few months later she told him that she would appreciate his hugs again. He said, "I guess you must be feeling better again," which gave her an opening to talk about her grief.

People who have been sexually wounded especially need a time of trust building before touching others and being touched. They need to know that at any time they can say no to any touch and be respected for setting this boundary. I provide counseling for people who were sexually molested as children. Some of them are afraid to go out in public, almost as if people could see the shame they carry for having been molested. One brave woman decided that she would push past her fear and go looking for a new church family. She nervously visited several churches to see what might happen. She was bombarded with hugs, unwanted handshakes, and a physical proximity that increased her anxiety. She became overwhelmed and each time left before the service was over. This is a person who needs a nonhugging congregation—or a congregation where people notice her posture, her downcast gaze, and her discomfort, and give her the space she needs.

When a woman came to a parish in the midst of a gender change, she sat in the back for a long while and ran out the door to her car directly after church. She wasn't sure she would be accepted. But gradually she let the smiles and respectful distance that other people honored draw her into their hearts. Now she sings in the choir and is an active leader in the congregation.

How can we know what kind of touch is appropriate? We let the other person guide us, and we let them stay as far away as they need to for as a long as they need to. We can tolerate various distances and the differences. We are a people of a tradition of respect who welcome those whom others have cast out. In every instance when Jesus healed an outsider, part of the cure was restoring that individual to loving community. A loving congregation honors individual difference, and respects touch boundaries—from the welcome of a parishioner at the start of the service to the benediction and departing. As we get to know one another, we find that we are all vulnerable adults in search of safety.

The Passing of the Peace

We need to pay attention to touch in worship, not only during informal times, such as gathering and departing, but in the more formal actions of the service itself. Do you greet one another on Sunday morning in worship with a time called "the passing of the peace?" Do you remember back in the 1970s when congregations first started implementing the practice? It was not an easy sell. In the old days, people were more proper in church and would never have thought about touching. Then in the '60s, amidst the free love movement, worship scholars retrieved the ritual of passing peace from earlier traditions. Clergy started making perfectly proper folks get up out of their seats and hug people. The resistance was intense.

Many worshipers in congregations have become comfortable with, or at least tolerant of, a certain style for passing the peace. To create a safe place for all worshipers, however, even those who would prefer not to touch, congregations need to reconsider this tradition and give worshipers permission not to touch.

So how do you pass the peace? Every change requires dialogue, compromise, and a willing leader. A pastor at a workshop suggested the following idea. She added this sentence to the worship bulletin: "I invite you to greet one another this morning by offering a bow, a handshake, or a hug. As we greet each other in different ways we offer these words: 'The peace of the Lord be with you,' and the response, 'and with your Spirit.'"

For a few weeks I tried a similar idea, with my own playful flare. I said, "This is the time in our service when we greet one another. So feel free to nod at someone, shake a hand, offer the politically safe and correct side hug, or, if you know someone really well (and have their permission), give 'em the old full body smash." Everyone laughed and started moving around. And what I noticed was that after church, people actually asked me if they could give me a hug before hugging me. They had gotten the message that some people may not want to be hugged, and that asking and noticing body postures is appropriate. My comments had taught them that different levels of relationship lead to different levels of physical contact. I was surprised and pleased at how easily they learned a new way to think about touching from this brief interaction in worship.

For Personal Reflection

What are some reasons that people do not want to be touched during the passing of the peace or similar rituals? Have you ever been in physical pain that limited your ability to hug or be hugged? If so, how did you respond? What are some things you could say to turn down someone's unwanted hug?

Blessings and the Laying On of Hands

Other worship practices offer opportunity for congregants to learn about touch. Many congregations have a healing ritual known as the laying on of hands; others use the laying on of hands for blessings and confirmation services. In my denomination this is usually done in the local church, but once a year we do it at our annual conference, a gathering of all of the clergy and key laity from around the region. Last year the bishop asked me to talk to the gathered Methodists about the "ask before you hug" curriculum that we were about to introduce throughout all of the churches.

Later that same day, the conference had a service of the laying on of hands for pastors who were commissioned to new places of service. The bishop, having taken a break during my speech, stood right up at the platform and told everyone to move closer to the people being commissioned and to lay hands on them. We all pushed our chairs back and throughout the hall surrounded the 25 individuals involved. Not wanting to miss an educational moment, however, I said really loudly to the pastor nearest to me, who was being smothered in touch, "Hey, there's a lot of people here with their hands all over you. Is that all right with you?" He responded with a loud and heartfelt yes. Had he not been comfortable, his only escape would have been to crawl under our legs and head for freedom.

I learned how much damage a ritual that includes touch can cause when I worked with Hmong immigrants in central California. As a dozen families prepared for new membership in the congregation I told them about the membership ritual, and that we usually ask the new member to kneel down and place our hands on his or her head. There was a stillness in the room that I could not understand. The leader of the group slowly told me that for his people the ritual would be offensive. "You see," he said, "when we were chased down and hunted by soldiers in the mountains they would force us to kneel down and place their hands on our heads just before they would shoot us." Asking them to kneel down would have triggered frightening and humiliating feelings for them. I thank God to this day that I had explained the tradition to them before we entered into it. That Sunday every new member stood proudly before us and without a single touch they were freely welcomed.

I know the powerful healing that can come through touch. I have personally received wonderful blessings through the laying on of hands. I also know that some of the people we surround with love in the laying on of hands feel overwhelmed by it and uncomfortable. In each instance of blessing or the laying on of hands, we must still take time to ask the person what his or her preference would be and offer alternatives. God works through the power of a circle of people holding hands. God works through our prayers and blessings, even if the person in the midst of our circle is standing alone, touched only by the Spirit's presence. Trusting God's healing work to happen in many ways, we provide alternatives to those for whom we pray.

Education for Church Meetings

In a clip from the film *Ask Before You Hug*,[3] a woman arrives late to a trustees meeting and the chairperson (a male) says, "Isn't that just like a woman to show up late." A few lines later he suggests that during the upcoming all-church workday, she make coffee in order to keep her nails from breaking. This is an illustration of a form of sexual harassment known as gender-directed behavior, as defined and discussed in the previous chapter. The effect on the woman in this situation was that she was left feeling demeaned, stereotyped, and unappreciated.

Gender-directed behavior in the church could involve leaders, members, or clergy. It can involve a one-time incident but most likely consists of a pattern of behavior. Gender issues in the church include the ratio of women to men in positions of power and on policy-making boards. Who is allowed to speak up and when may differ on the basis of gender. To determine the extent of gender differences in your congregation, ask questions such as the following:

- Are conversations that are deemed to too emotional squelched, thereby discouraging women to stay out of decision-making processes?
- Are people put in positions according to their gender (e.g., the women in education and the men on the building and grounds committee)?
- Does the congregation allow comments and jokes about one gender or another, or the capabilities of one gender as opposed to another?

These questions identify the elements of hostile environments, behaviors that fall within most standard definitions of sexual harassment. It is therefore of utmost concern in the prevention of sexual abuse that the issue of gender and gender-directed roles and behaviors be regularly considered.

Committee meetings are the most likely places for gender-directed behavior to become evident in our congregations and therefore are where we have the greatest opportunity to name and stop gender-directed behavior that could be considered sexual harassment. Behavior at meetings such as jokes, innuendo, sarcasm, stereotyping according to gender, and assigning individuals to roles based on gender all need to be reviewed. Once people become aware that their comments or touch behaviors are gender directed, they could be given tools to help them change.

For Personal Reflection

Do you ever feel angry about the way that someone comments on your gender? Have you felt angry when someone ignored a statement you made at a meeting? How do you communicate your feelings of anger to others? What might you have said if you were the woman who arrived late to the meeting?

Touch and Power

Educating the congregation about touch boundaries will likely reveal a still deeper issue: touching is sometimes about power, rather than care. When has a hug felt like a bribe to you? When have you behaved seductively in order to feel powerful? People who use touch as a way to gain power over others are being abusive. The touch can be as subtle as a hug and have the emotional feel of an arm-twisting. The story below will illustrate the way that a church leader used touch to keep everyone around her in a one-down position.

When Sarah arrived as pastor in a new parish, several members told her about a woman in the church who had too much power over everyone and used it to her advantage. A long-time leader in the church, the woman had been out of town for the installation and reception and missed meeting Sarah along with the others. One Saturday morning, Pastor Sarah arrived at the women's tea and Bible study. The church leader came into the room and immediately commanded everyone's attention. She was a large woman with a booming voice that took charge. Intuitively, Sarah, who was shorter and smaller than the woman, stood up and walked into the center of the room to meet her. Before she could do anything about it, the large woman had taken Sarah into her arms and was giving her a bear hug. Sarah found herself in such a tight hold that she could not breathe. Her adrenaline kicked in and her body and emotional system were set to fight off her attacker.

Sarah took the woman by the forearms, pushed her away to arm's length, and said, "I don't know you, and I don't want to be hugged like that. Please don't touch me again." When she regained her composure and realized what she had said, she was embarrassed and frightened. "What will they think of me? I've blown it now! What was I thinking?" Sarah envisioned the call she thought that she would soon receive from the head of the search committee: "Sarah, we've changed our mind." But this never happened. What did happen? For months after that, individuals in the congregation came up to Sarah in private and said, "I'm so glad that you did that. She's been trying to control the church for years and one of the ways she did that was by invading our space. None of us liked those hugs." Others said, "We sure needed someone to tell her to cut it out."

While the woman remained distant for most of Sarah's ministry, Sarah had actually accomplished what the congregation needed: she had placed a professional boundary between the woman, herself, and others in the congregation. Sarah's action had reduced the woman's power by redirecting the woman's touch behavior. The abuse of power and physical abuse too frequently go hand in hand. This is a clear example of the way in which touch is sometimes used to intimidate and minimize others. Stopping this behavior is a crucial step in making sure that the congregation makes respect and safety a priority.

We can both honor the value of touch and do it far more carefully. Every event in the life of the congregation provides people with opportunities in which to blunder into unwanted touch behaviors, or to engage consciously in touch behavior that is respectful. I invite you to analyze the touch behaviors around you and then learn and teach new touch behaviors.

Touch is only safe when it is freely chosen and mutually agreed upon by people of equal power and shared with the utmost care and respect. Loving words go a long way to establish relationships of agape at times when touch could be misunderstood or misinterpreted. When touch is risky or dangerous to another's body, soul, or psychic integrity, prayer is the touch that heals. Not touching can be as healing as touching. In multicultural ministry and with those who have been violated by touch, our commitment to keeping appropriate boundaries welcomes, liberates, and heals.

FIVE

Professional Roles and Romantic Relationships

Several issues regarding professional ministry and sexual abuse need particular attention. Clergy are involved in intimate moments in the lives of parishioners: at births and baptisms, in times of marital strife or divorce, when illness or tragedy strikes, and often at the end of life. Lay ministers, youth leaders, and pastoral counselors all share similar roles and professional responsibilities. Along with clergy, they are privileged to know secret or confidential information, including sexual and romantic concerns.

These issues must be handled with extreme care. Ironically, ministry professionals, who experience such great intimacy with people by virtue of their work, have been slow to develop ethical guidelines. It is crucial, however, that they learn how to handle intimacy, because without clear boundaries and training, they are vulnerable to developing inappropriately intimate relationships, including the using of the parishioner to unload personal frustrations, marital problems, or sexual issues. They may also become the recipient of someone's sexual advances, or cross sexual boundaries by using sexual innuendo, touch, or the exchange of sexual favors for advancement.

This chapter provides information that will help clergy and lay professionals lower their risk of being harassed and help them handle harassment. It also provides guidelines for ministry professionals about what to do when a parishioner expresses interest in a romantic, dating, or in any way sexualized relationship.

Sexual Advances

There may be times when a parishioner imagines that a romantic relationship with the pastor is possible. This could happen when a single person is interested in a more romantic or closer relationship with a single pastor. Whether the pastor is single or married, a parishioner may misconstrue the loving intimacy of the pastoral relationship, and begin to think of it as romantic love. It may happen because the clergy person consciously or unconsciously fosters a more mutually intimate relationship than is appropriate. It can also grow out of the projected desires of a parishioner who sees the pastor as an ideal mate because he or she is especially holy.

When the pastor is being pursued romantically or sexually by a lay member of the congregation who persists despite the pastor's clear statements of boundaries, it may be that the pastor is being sexually harassed. Anonymous surveys of clergywomen across denominations show that between 65 and 75 percent of clergywomen have experienced sexual abuse in the form of sexual harassment within their professional roles. This staggering number deserves our attention. My experience in workshops tells me that no fewer men are harassed, but more research is needed to verify this.

Sexual harassment toward a pastor may include intimidation of the pastor, giving gifts to the pastor with the hope that the pastor will respond with sexual or romantic attention, and stalking behaviors. The pastor may respond by withdrawal from ordinary ministry functions, exhibiting emotional distress, or experiencing a loss of self-efficacy. Without consultation and intervention this situation can become debilitating for the pastor and the congregation.

I was the victim of sexual harassment over a six-month period as the pastor of a rural community church. It began on that Christmas Eve when the man, whom I'll call Roger, waited until the end of the greeting line to speak to me about his attraction. I was shocked and silent. I hoped it was a temporary misstep on his part, perhaps brought on by too much eggnog or wassail. A week later Roger was in my office when I arrived at work. The secretary was apologetic. "I tried to tell him to wait elsewhere, but . . . (she shrugged her shoulders)." When I asked him what had brought him in to see me, he was vague. He seemed to make up something.

Roger continued to drop by at odd times, which was unnerving, to say the least. I lost focus on my work, and I was frequently scanning the horizon for his car or other evidence that he was somewhere around the building. Roger was in his seventies and married, so I hardly expected that he would actually continue to entertain the thought of a romantic relationship with me. I was a young mother and also married. Roger came by one day and told me that he wanted to help me and my husband buy a house so that we could "build a little equity." He told me that he would be glad to offer me a gift of about $50,000. That afternoon I called my district superintendent.

The superintendent seemed to think Roger's offer was a good idea and was dismissive about my concerns about Roger's other behaviors. None of us really understood or talked about the fact that this man was harassing me. I phoned another colleague, who was clearer about the issues. She asked, "What will he say you did to get that money?" That was all that it took. I told him flatly that I was not interested, and I also told him that I was not now and never would be interested in a personal relationship with him.

Roger continued to drop by the church at times when I was the only one in the building. He was polite yet demanding. He would make up reasons for needing to talk to me, and since he held a key position of power, the highest office that laity hold in my denomination, I felt that I had to deal with him. He called the office one day and asked me to visit him at his home that afternoon. He made a point of saying that his wife would not be home at that time. I did not make the requested home visit. About a week later I arrived for a meeting and parked my car, feeling relieved that no other cars were in the parking lot. As I rounded the corner to my office, Roger stepped out of the shadows and tried to hug me. I was faster and stronger, but he had made his emotional impact on me. At this point the situation was escalating, and I was in danger. He was not hearing me, or he did not like what he was hearing, so his behavior was getting worse.

I became distracted and dysfunctional at work. I was afraid to go to the office except when the secretary was there. I consulted my colleague again. She advised me to bring the man and his wife into my office to name the behavior, to show his wife my documentation of his every comment and behavior, and to demand that it stop. (Were I in this situation again, I would invite a member of the personnel committee to be present at the meeting. I would also obtain legal counsel regarding restraining and stalking orders and the filing of harassment or assault charges in court.)

Once Roger's wife was informed, Roger stopped his behavior. They also left the congregation, and while they were leaving, he made up lies to discredit my pastoral leadership. He told people that he was leaving because I had treated him badly. It was true that I had not renewed his position of leadership, because he had been using it to have power and control over me. But he told members only that I snubbed him by not giving him his rightful elected post. Members believed his stories, several families left the church, and my ministry was irreparably damaged.

Years later I spoke to the pastor who preceded me in that congregation. He told me that Roger had voted against accepting me as the pastor because of my gender. He had been adamant that a woman could not do a "man's" job. Harassment is often the result of underlying misogynistic agendas. Whether consciously or unconsciously, Roger found a way to intimidate me and to reduce my effectiveness in ministry. He had created a hostile work environment through his flirtations, manipulations, and verbal and physical abuse.

For Personal Reflection

How did you feel as you read this story? What parts of it can you relate to? If you were the pastor, what would you have done to stop Roger's behaviors? If you learned that this was happening to the pastor or rabbi of your congregation, what would you do?

Clergy Beware

Parishioners' expressions of sexual interest will not necessarily take the form of harassment. There is a real likelihood that someone in the parish will fall in love with a pastor or lay staff member. Clergy are attractive to lay people because they are trained to be careful, patient listeners—something for which many people are starved. If someone desires a closer relationship with God, a closer relationship with the pastor may be part of the plan. Those who feel particularly damaged and unworthy may seek out a relationship with someone particularly able to offer them grace or forgiveness. Both clergy and lay staff have an aura of holiness about them that parishioners may find sexually attractive.

Counseling situations are particularly rife with opportunities for confusion about the nature of the relationship. When counseling a member of the congregation, the pastor is often told, "Nobody else knows about this." The relationship can be charged with intimacy. As people develop a close relationship during pastoral counseling, they may also perceive that closeness as a romantic or sexual interest and wish it were fuller. In workshops I tell clergy, "At least think of yourself highly enough to prepare for the inevitable—that someone will become sexually attracted to you." When clergy watch scenes on videotape in which someone expresses sexual attraction toward a counselor, the room grows silent as it sinks in that this could happen to them, or as they recall a time when it did. Before long someone will break into that silence with laughter to relieve the tension. In the silence and in the laughter the discomfort is obvious.

It is terribly overwhelming to have someone express a sexual attraction toward you. A lot of feelings can arise. You might feel energized, flattered, attractive, aroused, confused, misunderstood, or even angry. Your instinct might be to run out the door. You might also want to do a little dance, or reach across the room and hug that person. I have no doubt that your body will be flooded with adrenaline. You will probably not be able to think clearly. Before doing anything, stop. Then think.

Handling Expressions of Sexual Interest

How should a professional respond to someone's expression of the desire for a romantic relationship? Let me put you into a scene that might actually happen. A person who has been coming to you for grief counseling tells you that he or she finds the sessions "rich and stimulating." The person then says, "I feel really awkward telling you this, but I've been having some, well, quite a few thoughts about you between our appointments. When I am with you [pause], I feel understood in such an intimate way, and I feel like God is right here in the room with us. I've been praying about this, and I've been thinking that maybe God wants us to draw even closer to each other in, well, you know, a romantic way. I know I'd really like that."

The professional should never indicate his or her interest in the romantic relationship. This would deepen the intimacy, immediately change the pastor's role, and increase the hope on one or both of their parts that a love relationship might be fulfilled. Since attraction is biochemical, both people probably have some good feelings taking them places they cannot fully control. Acknowledging these feelings gives the body permission to produce more of them and the psyche permission to create fulfillment fantasies. If the two people have a secret together, even more attraction can result. This is also biochemical. The arousal center in the brain responds to fear and to sexual attraction in the same way. When both are present, the "animal" is even more prepared to go through with the mating act.

Under no circumstance should a professional tell a parishioner about his or her sexual attraction to anyone. Remember that harassment includes the sharing of fantasies, sexual desires, and attractions that could be interpreted as coercive. Disclosing a sexual attraction, whether initiated or responded to by the professional, could be considered sexual harassment and abuse.

Here are specific steps you can take "in the heat of the moment" if a parishioner expresses interest in a sexual relationship. I have adapted these guidelines from the American Psychological Association's Psychotherapy Videotape Series on therapist's responses to the expression of sexual attraction in counseling.[1]

Step 1: Keep Silent

At that moment, you will have a lot to think about, and your feelings and physical responses will be on high alert. So, breathe deeply and be silent for a while. Picture God in the room with you. Notice and name your feelings to yourself at that moment. Accept them as they are.

Step 2: Accept the Parishioner's Feelings

The man or woman who has just approached you is also feeling a lot of things. It took courage to tell you about these feelings, and you now have a vulnerable person in your office. When you begin to speak, choose something in your first sentence that honors this person for telling you more about his or her life. For example, "Thank you for telling me about this. I bet it wasn't easy to do that." Or, "You've told me something very precious to you, and I honor that." These expressions ensure that the person who disclosed to you is not shamed for truth telling or made to look like a lovesick fool.

Step 3: Validate the Relationship

You can tell the person that you find the relationship important as well. This must be done carefully, so as not to convey mutual interest in a different type of relationship. You could say, for example, "I am honored to be your pastor [or lay counselor], and I'm glad that you have found this time helpful." You could say, "Sometimes caring and connection can lead to feelings of romantic interest or to sexual feelings, and that's understandable." In your next sentence you can define the limited professional nature of this relationship.

Step 4: Clarify the Professional Boundary

At this point you need to make several statements that make it clear that the two of you are in a professional relationship. "I'm glad that you feel that coming into the office is helpful to you. There are a few things I need you to know. First, that it would be inappropriate [or unethical] for me to have a romantic or dating relationship with anyone in the parish. Because I am the professional in this relationship, I have an unfair power advantage in it—we are not equals here." Now you need to draw the line in the sand that you will not cross over: "I never develop romantic relationships with parishioners. That's a hard and fast rule of mine." If your church has a policy about professional boundaries, this would be a good time to cite it.

Step 5: Pause for Response

Ask how the person is responding to what you have said. Listen for clues that he or she has really understood. If you are not sure, state your position once again. Answer questions. Restate your position as many times as necessary until you are sure that you have been understood. Your parishioner may or may not want to continue to see you after this conversation. You can clarify that before ending the conversation.

Further Steps for Responding

Do you want to set another appointment with this person? If you are uncertain, consult a colleague or professional counselor. If you have set the boundary and you feel confident that both of you will respect it, you would naturally set another appointment. Make sure that nothing changes about the appointment frequency, duration, or place. I recommend meeting at a time when there are other people in the building and preferably in an office with a small glass window. An ideal office layout would be to arrange the furniture in the office so that the pastor or counselor can be seen through the window, but the other person cannot be.

If you have decided that you cannot continue to be an unbiased professional in this situation, refer this person to a counselor or another pastor in the community, so that he or she can continue to get grief counseling without the awkwardness of the relationship issue getting in the way. You have an ethical obligation to uphold the profession, set the boundary, and respond with compassion. You are not obliged to hear more lengthy statements of romantic interest (this would begin to be harassment of you). You are not obliged to counsel anyone when an attraction interferes with your ability to maintain focus on the person's best interest and leave your own thoughts, feelings, and attractions out of the relationship.

If the Situation Is Extreme

In the event that the situation involves the parishioner removing clothing, making physical contact with the clergy person, or using overt sexual language or behavior, the steps just outlined will not be adequate. If any of these things occur, the clergy person is in danger and the following steps would be better used. Tell the person directly that the behavior has to stop, and that you are leaving the room. Tell the person that you must now break the confidential nature of the interaction because it has become sexual harassment or a sexual assault. Bring the office volunteer or secretary into the room with you when you reenter it. Ask the witness to document exactly what each of you say as you clarify the situation and describe specifically which behavior has to stop. You may let the person know that the behavior constitutes sexual harassment and that you will consider (or take) legal action if necessary to be sure that it stops. In this case you would clearly not see the individual again in person and you would refer this person to a therapist for intervention.

Whether or not the situation is extreme, I urge you to document conversations as soon as possible. Document the time and place and write a narrative of what was said. Keep it in a confidential place, and consider sharing a copy of it with a professional consultant. You may need to inform someone on the personnel committee about the situation, especially if the parishioner's expressions of romantic interest continue.

For Personal Reflection

When have you documented the actions or comments of others? How did you feel about doing that? Clergy need to have established a relationship with a professional colleague or therapist to consult in times like these. Do you know if your pastor or rabbi (or have you, if you are clergy) established such a relationship? If not, why not?

Responding to Harassment

Clergy need to know how to handle the primarily healthy individual who expresses sexual or romantic interest, and how to handle more extreme forms of sexual harassment. In a situation like the one I experienced with Roger, as I said, I would do things quite differently today. I would make sure that any congregation I serve has a current policy on sexual abuse that defines harassment and establishes consequences for such behavior. I would consult a therapist or colleague about the situation. I would provide my documentation to the chairperson of the personnel committee, and ask for help in determining further interventions. I would inform key lay leaders about any situation of harassment while it was being handled and afterward, so that destructive rumors could be countered by the truth.

I would speak carefully about the situation with trusted congregants. Harassment is real psychological abuse that deeply affects victims. Clergy left to handle such situations alone can end up damaged for a long time, some of them leaving the profession altogether. I know that the stress of this situation on me is one of the reasons that I am so passionate about abuse prevention. We do not hear of these situations often, because so many clergy still live under those no-talk rules. Women and men who are victims of harassment are often silent, delaying the process of getting help and healing.

Consensual Relationships and Power

Sexualized contact between a pastor and a parishioner in the context of the ministerial role is never consensual because the clergy person has more power in the relationship. The clergy or staff person could be viewed as sexually harassing the parishioner. The ministerial role includes the daily activities of a pastor in a congregation, such as calling on parishioners, preaching, teaching, counseling, office work, the administration of programs, and conducting worship. In any of these roles a sexualized relationship is not consensual with a child, an adolescent, or an adult, due to the power inherent within the pastoral role. Pastoral responsibilities may also include ministries beyond the local church, such as chaplaincy or pastoral counseling, and specialized duties, such as the supervision of ministerial candidates. Just as there is always a power difference between a minister and a parishioner, a supervisor always has power over a ministerial candidate.

Among all of the helping professionals, the clergy role is highly charged with power and authority. The nature of the profession can easily cause a person to project onto the clergy an expectation of saintliness. The pastor is an authority on the word of God and on the "truth." The pastor is the teacher of the Bible and is seen as holding the key to spiritual well-being. The rabbi is looked up to as a person with a direct link to God.

While these projections onto clergy are particularly strong, lay staff members also carry some of these roles and qualities. They too possess more power and status than their congregants. Thus, there is a power difference between a mentor and a student, a spiritual leader and a disciple, a trained lay minister and a parishioner, a Sunday school superintendent and a teacher.

When someone comes to the church in search of spiritual services or counseling, he or she is looking for relationships within a community in which to explore faith and life issues. The pastor or lay staff member becomes a counselor, teacher, scriptural interpreter, and spiritual mentor. These are all professional roles of power and authority. The pastor or staff member's perception that he or she is *not* a person of power does not mean that the relationship is equal. The pastor's desire for an equal relationship does not mean that the relationship is equal. Those who seek counseling in the congregation are in the less powerful role. Therefore a sexualized relationship between clergy or lay staff and volunteers cannot be consensual, because contact between a pastor or lay minister and parishioner is inherently unbalanced. Flirting, sexual language, sexual jokes, and sexualized touch are exploitative when there is an inherent power difference between a professional and someone who is being served.

Single Pastors and Ethical Concerns

In the recent past, it was rightly assumed that almost all Protestant clergy were married. Today the divorce rate among clergy is nearly as high as that in the general population, and many seminary students are second-career singles. As sexuality-related risks inherent in the clergy role are being discussed, another factor must be considered: congregational expectations about the appropriate sexual behavior for single clergy.

More and more denominational and local church policies prohibit the pastor from dating someone in the congregation. Because of the power differential described above, it is an ethical violation for a pastor to approach parishioners as potential dating partners or mates. But what can be done to provide single pastors who seek partnership the opportunities to meet people outside of the parish? Often single pastors need to travel to nearby communities to be with friends or persons they are dating and to get away from the fishbowl life of the pastor.

The role of congregational pastor is often a lonely role. Single clergy who have a sufficient support system beyond the parish are nourished and upheld in their work. Others, with limited time to establish friendships, evening meetings that limit their abilty to meet potential partners, and feeling themselves under the watchful eyes of parishioners when they do date, experience grief and burnout. A pastor who devotes the majority of his or her time to work in the congregation may think that he or she has little opportunity to meet and date people beyond the parish. Yet single clergy are drawn to the very people they are not allowed to date: the people in congregations who understand and support their ministry.

Even relationships that seem quite natural may be inherently unethical and carry significant risk. Suppose, for example, that Carol, a newly single woman, begins attending a congregation. During the year following her divorce, Carol seeks the counsel of her pastor, a single man about her age. She is emotionally tender during this time, and her self-esteem is understandably quite low. What are the risks in this scenario? First, we have already established that a relationship between Carol and her pastor cannot be consensual, because by virtue of his role, the pastor has more power in the relationship. The pastor cannot ethically be in the dual roles of counselor and love interest. Second, because Carol is dealing with significant wounds right now, her ability to exercise good judgment is compromised. In fact, it seems reasonable to assume that she could indiscriminately attach to a new man who expresses compassion for her in this time of upheaval. A third risk has practical ramifications: If the relationship does not pan out, one of them will probably have to leave the congregation. Even if Carol's need for love is directed toward her pastor, the pastor must lovingly redirect her to other relationships. His role as a pastoral counselor is to help Carol process her loss, regain a sense of self-worth and hope, and strengthen her walk with God.

What happens when a single pastor and a single parishioner develop a mutual attraction? Some congregations have handled such situations by urging the parishioner to attend another parish or nearby congregation. She or he would leave the congregation so that they could date each other. In multiple-staff situations, the parishioner may be able to maintain a relationship with another pastor on staff for pastoral needs, while dating a person who is a visitor to or member of the congregation. Attempts to solve the issue of the power difference between them may or may not be effective.

For Personal Reflection

How would you feel if your pastor or rabbi was dating someone in the congregation? Do you believe that this person has the same rights to privacy that other members of the congregation have? Would any dating guidelines protect the congregation from the possibility of a harassment lawsuit? What guidelines, policies, or changes in policy would you suggest for your own congregation?

The ethical guidelines of some helping professions prohibit dating relationships for a minimum of two years following the time when the two had a professional relationship, and then only if the professional contact was limited, extremely brief, and occurred at a time when the client was not particularly vulnerable.[2] Careful review of these issues is required and standards of practice on this issue are evolving. Clergy are advised to document their concerns, to consult clergy colleagues, and to inform superintendents or other judicatory staff when questions arise.

Changing Times

Congregations have been lenient in the area of single clergy relationships with parishioners because they have not acknowledged the power imbalance between a minister (lay or clergy) and a member of a congregation. Whether the pastor is counseling the parishioner or not, the role of spiritual leader, clergy or lay, has within it a professional standard not unlike that of doctor, psychologist, and teacher. All of these professions have ethical codes prohibiting romantic and dating relationships between these professionals and the people they serve.

These comments are in no way intended to place blame or bring shame on pastors who in the past have dated and married parishioners. The desire of a pastor to date an active member of the faith is understandable. Many of those relationships developed in the absence of policies, training, and ethical guidelines. Congregations have been notoriously inclined to assist the pastor in finding an appropriate spouse within the congregation.

At one time it was expected that pastors be married when they arrived at congregations, although they had been prohibited from dating when they were seminarians, and a pastor who arrived without a wife was expected to find one in the congregation pronto! In fact, in the late 1940s, a pastor in a small-town church was run out of town for *not dating* the most eligible and rich widow whom his congregation had chosen for him!

Even today, congregations love to meddle in and gossip about a single pastor's affairs. Congregations need to discuss this dynamic within broader discussions about the establishment of professional and ethical guidelines. We need an educated pool of clergy, lay staff, and volunteer leaders who understand the dangers inherent in dating relationships and the possibility of lawsuits related to sexual harassment. We need to educate clergy, staff, volunteers, and members of the congregation about ethical boundaries through policy statements, articles in newsletters, and workshops.

The Resulting Damage

Congregations that have lived through sexual harassment suffer from its insidious affects. The community becomes distracted from vital mission and ministry programs. The esteem of the congregation plummets. The individual members who are involved are wounded, and therefore, the whole body of Christ is wounded. Some congregations end up losing members; others eventually close.

Current, well-developed policies establish ethical boundaries and prevent harassment. Quick thinking and decisive action on the part of clergy and laity can stop unwanted and inappropriate behavior before it escalates and, we hope, before others are harmed by it. Remember that harassment is not simply about sexuality—it's also about power. Training and education are key. Policies can raise awareness as you create respectful, safe communities.

SIX

Congregations at Risk

Congregations have people within them who have precarious psychological conditions. This chapter explores those conditions: sexual shame, sexual addiction, addiction to pornography, romantic delusion, and unhealed victims of sexual abuse who become perpetrators.

Sexual Shame in the Congregation

Is your congregation a place where sexually wounded people find healing? In healthy environments, people experience a restoration of their lives by association with others who are nonjudgmental. Can people who have wounds and injuries about their sexual fantasies, behaviors, orientation, or abuse find healing in your congregation? When congregations and pastors openly discuss sexual issues, recognize and honor the complexity of sexuality, and talk about sexual issues, a "no shame zone" is created for individuals with sexual wounds.[1]

Imagine for a moment that you have experienced a traumatic sexual experience in your past. This may be a real experience, rather than an imaginary one, depending on your life journey. Say that you have some sexual experience you have rarely or never talked about with anyone. You feel a sense of shame about these experiences and may not want to talk about them. So you find a congregation where issues of sexuality are hush-hush. The only problem with this is that the silence reinforces your feelings that this sexual experience has rendered you unworthy, dirty, or unholy in the sight of God. You sought out the church while hiding your sexual problems and yet this hiding, in effect, makes you worse. Sexual shame hides beneath secrets and the secrets themselves create more shame.

People who are hiding sexual secrets are among the most vulnerable of individuals. They can more easily become victims of sexual boundary violations or may be perpetrators of sexual abuse. The silence and secrets that these individuals keep contribute to their personal shame and can erupt into the life of the congregation without warning.

Congregations that reinforce sexual shame by their silence or by condemning people for a whole host of sexual "sins" are places where sexually ashamed people feel at home. The congregation's responses to sexuality issues may be similar to the responses shamed individuals were given at home as children and adolescents. They may act out and injure others in response to the congregation's parental judgment and censorship.

Reviewing Congregational History

How can your congregation determine whether or not it reinforces sexual shame? You need to begin by asking about the sexual secrets in your congregation. Congregations with secrets provide a container in which sexual shame can ferment. By contrast, open and healthy congregations have learned to talk safely about former secrets and the damage they created, and have taken corrective measures. I urge you to assess the level of sexual shame in your congregation by completing a church-family history to determine what sexual secrets have affected the congregation. You will then need to encourage open discussion about that history.

A pastor, upon arriving at his new congregation, sat on the floor in a meeting and rolled out a large section of newsprint on the floor in the midst of a group of lay leaders. Together they drew a line that represented the history of the church and noted high points and low points in the history of the congregation. They sketched in the successes and some of the failures. Eventually the pastor asked them to add the secrets that the congregation had kept. If they could not say them out loud they were invited to simply write them down or illustrate them on the paper. This process led them to a remarkably honest appraisal of the congregation and its families. They began talking about things that they had previously covered up, such as the story of the pastor who committed suicide in the basement of the old parsonage, the affair that one of the pastors had, children they knew about who had suddenly left the church because their dad was put in jail for having molested them. They talked about an incidence of sexual abuse that had taken place in the congregation in the not-too-distant past. They talked together about how they felt, what they had done about the abuse, and how the secret might still be affecting the congregation today. Taking a congregational history in this way fostered a spirit of openness among the lay leadership and the pastor. This pastor's method is one good example of the many ways that a congregation could talk about and address past secrets and congregational shame.

> *For Personal Reflection*
>
> What are the highlights of your church's history? The turning points? The low points? The secrets? Can you think of another way to help your congregation fully review its history?

The Consequence of Silence

After years of silence on sexual issues, a congregation can sometimes become stuck in a place of shame. When sexual boundaries are crossed in a congregation, the feelings of shame associated with this problem can linger for years in what we could call the personality of the congregation. Congregations, like our families of origin, may become mired in sexual shame, and they too can develop low self-esteem, depression, and emotional diseases. When congregations hide and cover up sexual issues or secrets, they tend to acquire rigid thinking patterns and vacillate between blame and shame (the two polar ends of the same affect). They often become fearful and controlling. The whole congregational system uses up vital energy to protect the secret, monitor what is said about the secret, and to keep potential "whistle blowers" silent.[2] When a new pastor or new members come into such a congregation, they are encouraged to join in the conspiracies of silence under the guise of protecting individuals and keeping the image of the congregation as a whole from being tarnished.

Congregations that keep sexual secrets tend to be magnets for people with sexual shame. Individuals who have been raped, people with impotency issues, people who have borne children and given them over to be adopted, people who are sexually addicted, people who have sexually abused others or been sexually abused may carry sexual shame. People who feel damaged and unworthy in the sight of God may unconsciously look for a congregation that articulates their shame. Unfortunately, choosing another environment of shame may not be restorative or healing because it simply reinforces unworthiness.

People who were told by their families that it is not okay to talk about sex and that sex is dirty and disgusting often find that this message is reinforced theologically. Perhaps they were told that God or Jesus condemns them because they masturbate, or that they will go to hell for having had sex before marriage. If they believed this message, they feel comfortable in a congregation that confirms their unworthiness in the sight of God. People who have not addressed those old messages in a healthy way, could try to test their new congregational family—to see whether or not it is okay to talk about sex. They might even challenge sexual boundaries to see what would happen.

People who have grown up in homes where they were shunned because of their gender or sexual orientation have to restore their sense of self-worth outside of that original family. Some of them seek a congregation that will love them without stigma or shame, possibly pushing the limits of people's comfort with them as a way of testing out the new environment. They might find a congregational family and challenge that family to accept them, because their family of origin never did. An open and accepting congregation provides essential healing for people whose families have rejected them.

Where Shame Begins

Sexual shame begins in the family. It begins with parents who, due to their own culture or experiences, are not comfortable talking about body parts or bodily functions, and go out of their way to avoid discussing sexuality. Children can intuitively pick up on their parent's attitudes about subjects they discuss, and they can feel a parent's embarrassment even when words are not spoken.

Shame is often transmitted indirectly. It may begin when a girl is told not to hang upside down on a jungle gym because the boys will look at her panties. It may begin when a boy sees his mother's shocked response to finding a dirty magazine under his bed, or when a preteen daughter is scolded for something that was not a problem before she entered puberty, such as wearing her pajamas around the house. It sneaks into the souls of 12- and 13-year-olds when their parents accuse them of being too interested in sex. Many people still remember early adolescent sexual experiences that they were told were disgusting or dirty. Parents have too often said, "You should be ashamed of yourself." Many good parents express shame or disgust about sexuality and adolescent sexual behaviors in an attempt to protect their children without understanding the lingering consequences of shame. Some women carry shame into their adult years about their physical appearance or adolescent "promiscuity." Some men carry shame about their erotic responses to visual images and about times when they pressured someone into having sex with them. Feeling self-loathing about any aspect of sexual orientation, experience, or abuse has lasting effects on self-esteem, relationships, and spirituality.

Almost everyone comes through life with some experience of shame. Shame is different than guilt. Guilt is a feeling of remorse about a mistaken behavior and can be corrected by behavior. Shame is a deeper more pervasive experience that one's very core self is flawed. The guilty person says, "I made a mistake." The ashamed person says, "I am a mistake." In many families of origin, behavior and value are fused. A wrong behavior is seen as a character flaw. The person with shame feels that he or she is not redeemable despite corrective actions.

Victims of Sexual Abuse

Some of us acquire sexual shame by our parents' nonverbal cues; others acquire shame from specific behaviors, including abuse. As many as one in three girls and one in ten boys has been sexually abused by age 18. The abuse rate is higher for people with disabilities. In families where molestation takes place, the boys are as likely to be abused as the girls are. The shame that a victim of sexual abuse feels is often carried silently, secretly, for long periods of time. Once the story is told and healing processes are put in place, the shame often still lingers. The victim feels shame for simply having been there as a witness and participant. The sense of lost cleanliness and holiness is the hardest aspect of a person's life to heal following sexual abuse.

Researchers of sexuality have found that many girls involved in sexual molestations as children have higher levels of interest in sexual activity as teens. They prematurely develop hormonal and other biochemical readiness for sexual activity. These are the girls that have been labeled "tramp" and "whore." They are doubly wounded when they are ostracized for becoming sexually active as adolescents.[3] Youth who have been abused may act out through drug and alcohol use or turn inward and withdraw socially. Others may act out sexually, and in that case their sexual shame is reinforced by parents, youth leaders, and their peers.

> ***For Personal Reflection***
>
> When as a child did you feel shame? As a teenager? As an adult? Did you hide your shame with silence, withdrawal, obsessions, addictions, acing out, bravado, or other coping mechanisms? Think of an area of sexual shame that you carry from the past. How would you go about healing it?

Those who were sexually shamed at an early age through incest or other sexual abuse make a recovery journey that requires time and skilled intervention. They are among those who come to the church to find healing. If they have not healed, they may put themselves, pastors and lay staff, and members of the congregation at risk. They may remain emotionally dependent on the pastor or congregation. Feeling powerless, they may unconsciously seek the attention, even the sexual attention, of others. They may behave seductively in order to have someone reenact their childhood trauma with them. For example, an unhealthy abuse victim may view the pastor as a similar person to his or her abusive parent. Abuse victims have been taught confusing messages about sexual boundaries and cannot always distinguish the difference between love and sex. Clergy who are unaware of these dynamics may not set clear boundaries and could mistake an unhealthy sexual overture for true romantic attraction. Clergy can become potential victims themselves when former victims try to reenact past abuse.

A Youth Pastor's Dangerous Encounter with an Abuse Victim

In a congregation such as yours, an adolescent who had been sexually abused became seductive. Sara's story illustrates the way that unhealed victims may victimize others by acting out, seduction, false reporting, or obsessions.

At age 16, Sara was fond of the college-age youth director at her church. She dropped by his office after school a couple of days each week, and she talked to him about her life in an open manner. He was a good listener. She thought of him as the good father she never had. Her real father drank a lot of alchohol after work every day and started having sex with her when she was 11. When she was 12 her mother divorced him, and Sara was free of his abuse. But Sara remained psychologically confused about love and sexual intimacy. She was flirtatious with the boys in the youth group and especially so with the youth director. He took this as flattery and believed that it was normal adolescent behavior—until one night when he gave Sara a ride home after group. At a stoplight she leaned toward him and kissed his ear. When the light changed and as he continued driving, Sara took off her shirt and asked him to pull the car over. Sara was unconsciously reenacting her own abuse, trying to get him to cross a boundary with her. By seducing the youth pastor, she would get him to behave as her father had. Sarah wanted the youth pastor to love her the way her father had, never understanding the difference between love and sexual abuse.

All children assume their parents love them, so throughout their lives, when they seek love, they will look for the familiar form of love they received from their parents. If their parents abused them, they will unconsciously assume that love looks like abuse. They will seek abusive relationships and act out to create relationships that feel familiar. Sexual abuse victims may confuse sexual aggression with seduction and seduction with love. That is what Sara was unconsciously doing.

The youth pastor did not touch Sara, but she aroused him and she knew it. He got out of the car and left her there while he sat on the curb trying to think about what to do. He was in real trouble with a very troubled teen.

Sara got dressed while he cooled off, and she leaned her head out the window and apologized to him. He trusted her apology and got back into the car and drove her home. But he knew that she could say anything to anyone about what had happened, and if she was mad at him (a projection of her anger toward her father), she could ruin his job at the church or possibly file charges against him. The youth pastor never talked about the situation and soon thereafter resigned without explanation.

The congregation never learned anything from his experience, because it was not discussed. There were no policies in place that addressed sexual behaviors, nor had the congregation provided the youth pastor with training about how to handle such a situation. They had left him in a vulnerable position by failing to create a guideline that two unrelated adults must be in the car whenever youth are transported. He was reasonably afraid to bring it up and thought that if he did, the senior pastor or the personnel committee might accuse him of having initiated the contact. Had he been trained in risk prevention, he probably would not have been in this terrifying situation. Or when he found himself in such a situation, he might have trusted a colleague or the personnel committee with the story.

The Consequences of Sexual Secrets

After the youth pastor left, the congregation was still left with a sexual secret. The youth pastor's lack of disclosure about the incident meant that the next person in his position would be at risk with Sara too. She was never given the opportunity to heal, and his shame about the incident lingered in the collective unconscious of the community. He went away carrying his shame about it to his next parish, and never had the opportunity to learn from the trauma or understand what happened to him. If he tried to block out his thoughts and emotions rather than learning from them, something similar could happen to him at a later time.

Whether as pastor or laity, people want sexual healing and come to faith communities in the hope of finding it at the font, the table, and in fellowship. The healing cannot take place for individuals or congregations as long as shame is reinforced. Unfortunately, most faith communities approach sexuality from the perspective of hard and fast rules and rigid norms. Some of us were taught that sex is only pure and holy under specific and limited circumstances, primarily in married heterosexual relationships. People whose sexual behavior falls outside of this norm remain silent about other sexual behaviors because of the disapproval of others. The most vocal opponents of sexual practices considered deviant may have shame about those exact practices from personal experiences with them.

Congregations can and do act similarly to families with secrets. In a form of denial, they assume no "deviant" sexual behavior is taking place within their faith community. They limit conversations about sexuality, including sexual ethics, norms, and boundaries. They may also rigidly define acceptable sexual behaviors and focus on a few sexual "sins" to the exclusion of others—condemning some sexual behaviors while overlooking other unethical behaviors.

Like other families, the church family or synagogue has within it incest perpetrators, pedophiles, people who have been sexually traumatized, people addicted to pornography, and people with other sexual experiences that create and reinforce shame. Also among the leaders and members of the congregation are people with shame-based psychological disorders. Gershen Kaufman, author of *The Psychology of Shame*, refers to groups of disorders as "distinct syndromes of shame."[4] Many personality disorders are the result of sexual abuse. The person with a narcissistic personality covers inner shame with an outer cloak of holiness. The person with a dissociative disorder likely became psychologically dis-integrated during early childhood sexual abuse as a defense against the intensity of the trauma. People with masochistic disorders may have developed the condition from childhood abuse where they learned to submit to an angry, hostile abuser because they had no choice. I have briefly described only a few of the many dysfunctional mental health conditions that result from early childhood sexual trauma and abuse.[5]

For Personal Reflection

Think of people you know who have experienced sexual abuse. What has helped them move toward healing? What has prevented them from moving toward healing? How has their involvement in a faith community helped or hindered their healing?

When sexual abuse victims keep their suffering a secret (whether from themselves or others) they are in danger of becoming perpetrators. Many, but not all, sex offenders were themselves abused as children. Some studies indicate that as many as two-thirds of criminal sex offenders were abuse victims. Reports about the pedophilia epidemic in the Catholic Church point to two and three generations of priests who were sexually abused and then became abusers. Sexual abuse is passed down from one generation to another in families, in religious orders, and in congregations.

When the Victim Becomes the Perpetrator

Congregations are at risk when sexual abuse victims become sex addicts or sex abusers. Many sexual abuse survivors can and do recover and lead joyful and abundant lives. Variations in the length of time the person was abused, the age of the victimization, and resilience factors in the family and individual all contribute to how individuals cope with the abuse. But some people with childhood wounds, such as the young woman who tried to get the youth pastor to abuse her sexually, continue to find themselves—or even create for themselves—ongoing abusive situations. Other victims of child sexual abuse take on the role of perpetrator of sex abuse and abuse others.

You can understand that some people who have been sexually abused think of themselves as irreparably damaged. People who believe that this broken state is impossible to heal will repeat bad behaviors, because they think that they cannot do any more damage to themselves than has already been done.

Sexual abuse victims who become perpetrators have overwhelming and usually unacknowledged emotional shame. An individual who was sexually abused and felt confused, angry, sad, and powerless may reenact the abuse behavior in the role of the perpetrator. The victim-turned-perpetrator once saw his or her own perpetrator as a powerful person who derived pleasure from a forced sexual encounter. The unconscious voice of the victim-turned-perpetrator says, "Maybe it was fun to be the perpetrator" or "Maybe this time when I do it, I'll be the one in charge." Often perpetrators are so far cut off from their feelings and thoughts that they do not recognize that they are participating in abuse. The person feels out of control and watches scenes unfold, as would a cameraperson on a film crew. This cutting-off of the self that originally took place when the perpetrator was victimized can remain a lifetime pattern that allows him or her to act without feeling or thinking at times of emotional overload. It is a coping mechanism that goes awry.

Feelings of sadness, fear, panic, betrayal, and rage are difficult for the abuse victim to deal with. They are, in fact, stored in the brain without language in the right hemisphere where emotion is stored without language. At the time of abuse, the normal function of the brain is overwhelmed. Thoughts and feelings of the experience never move from the brain's right hemisphere to the left, where they could be made sense of as language or story. The trauma victim is left with a mass of emotions that make little sense and are not easily controlled by conscious thought. Until this residue of emotion is brought to consciousness and is worked through, it can erupt as emotional reaction, inaction, or impulsive action.

People who have healed sexual wounds in their lives through counseling, a lovingly restorative relationship, or other processes of change do not repeat the role of either victim or perpetrator. Telling the story of the abuse to someone safe is crucial. Those who have not sought help and those who have concurrent mental-health conditions such as mood disorders or psychotic disorders are at greatest risk for distorted sexual behaviors. Some abuse survivors turn to drugs or alcohol, develop eating disorders, or suffer other mental and physical conditions as they attempt to mask the pain.[6]

Sexual Addiction in the Congregation

Sexual addiction is another condition that puts clergy, laity, and congregations at risk. Like other addictions, sexual addiction is self-destructive behavior. The out-of-control sexual behavior can include high-risk sexuality, multiple partners, using prostitutes, voyeurism (including obsessive pornography use), and sexually abusing children or adults. The addiction is defined by the ways that these behaviors interfere with daily functioning, the amount of time involved in seeking sexual highs, and the degree of the risks that are taken. The consequences of addictive sexual behavior include a spiraling down of the person's mental health into depression, shame, and despair. The consequences can include one or more destroyed relationships, the loss of a job, arrest, becoming infected with one or more sexually transmitted diseases, criminal behavior, and even suicide.

I can imagine that you may be uncomfortable with this subject and wish that we did not have to dig into it very far. We have left issues such as these out of our conversations under the guise that they are private issues and that they should be left up to individual families to handle and heal. We would prefer to think that they do not exist among the people of our congregations. But they do.

Internet pornography places sexual materials at everyone's fingertips. This accessible information has become such a problem that John Bradshaw, a pioneer in the issue of family secrets and sexual shame, is now traveling the country providing workshops on the problem of pornography addiction. We who are leaders in congregations need to increase our awareness that sexual addictions damage individuals, couples, families, and congregations.

Sexual addiction involves a number of complex factors including biology, biochemistry, and social conditioning. While congregations have addressed issues of addiction to alcohol, gambling, and food, we have not yet acknowledged or addressed the problem of sexual addiction. Patrick Carnes, psychologist and expert in the area of sexual addiction, notes 10 signs of the presence of sexual addiction:[7]

1. A pattern of out-of-control behavior
2. Severe consequences due to sexual behavior
3. Inability to stop despite adverse consequences
4. Persistent pursuit of self-destructive or high-risk behavior
5. Ongoing desire or effort to limit sexual behavior
6. Sexual obsession and fantasy as a primary coping strategy
7. Increasing amounts of sexual experience because the current level of activity is no longer sufficient
8. Severe mood changes around sexual activity
9. Inordinate amounts of time spent in obtaining sex, being sexual, or recovering from sexual experience
10. Neglect of important social, occupational, or recreational activities because of sexual behavior

Feelings of shame that accompany sexual addiction are intense and lead to carefully constructed denial, interpersonal ineffectiveness, loss of self-esteem, estrangement from others, and the cutting off of connection to God. While longing for intimacy, the person with a sexual addiction loses healthy connection to others. The addict objectifies his or her desire and satisfies the addiction by objectifying others. Keeping a distance from others and seeing them as objects instead of people is a psychological process that sets the stage for abuse. A person who can no longer empathize with the recipient of sexual behavior is a dangerous person. Conversely, the ability to see the experience from the other's viewpoint is crucial to curbing the strong desires that lead to sexual abuse.

Congregations have growing numbers of sexually addicted clergy. A judicatory leader recently asked me to make a presentation at a conference on sexual addiction because several pastors in his area had been discovered to be spending hours on their computers viewing pornography and in chat rooms. A pastor in another area was arrested for child abuse because he had been communicating with an underage girl.

For Personal Reflection

What is your experience of viewing pornography on the Web? If you learned that a friend or coworker was using the computer more than an hour a day, how would you bring up the question of a possible sexual addiction? If you have children, how do you protect them from Internet pornography?

The Problem of Cybersex

Although sexual addicts, clergy or laity, have always found a variety of ways to feed their addictions, the ever-expanding world of cyberspace has provided a whole new arena for compulsive behavior. Clergy—and others—for whom sex has been especially taboo can now easily find information via the Internet. This eliminates the risk that bothersome neighbors will check the pastor's mailbox and discover magazines wrapped in brown paper. It eliminates the even higher risk of finding multiple partners or prostitutes with whom to satisfy sexual cravings. Since Internet sex can be viewed in the privacy of one's home or late at night in one's office, it is viewed in supposed safety. What appears to be safe access to sexual material is far from safe, however.

While many people look at pictures of naked people or pictures of people having sex from time to time, most people are not obsessive or compulsive about it. They are able to use it or not, and their use of it does not interfere with relationships, work, or other activities. Internet Web sites are being designed in such a way that they lead people who would not otherwise have used pornography into distorted and unsatisfying sexual addictions. These Web sites provide a strong behavioral process known as "intermittent reinforcement" to get customers to continue using the site. If you find a picture (i.e., "win") every now and then, you are more likely to keep playing than if you "win" every time. You are rewarded intermittently. This fuels an instinctual desire to look again. Perhaps this time a picture will be more revealing, the scene more arousing.

Individuals experience a powerful psychological reinforcement for such behaviors. The consequences of the use of these sites can include hours on the Internet—to the point of not eating, neglecting relationships, neglecting the home or personal hygiene, and even job loss.

Internet pornography is not safe for other reasons as well. The use of Internet pornography may lead to anonymous sex in chat rooms, including illegal conversations with minors about sex. It can lead to cruising, anonymous partners, and one-night stands. It can lead to other forms of sexual addiction, including paying for sex on the phone or in person, trading sexually explicit tapes and photographs, voyeurism, exhibitionism, sexual activity that involves pain, or sex with harmful objects. The use of the Internet has increased sexual activity directed toward and involving children. The presence of a child in a room where a computer is showing explicit sexual material is considered child abuse in most states.

Sexual addictions are powerful. The addict goes in search of the highs, and finding them, continues the behavior. But the behavior itself creates an ever-lowered sense of self-worth, and therefore the cycle begins. The addict thinks, "I feel ashamed of myself," and then because of these low feelings is even more drawn to repeat the behavior to achieve more of a high.

The person who has overwhelming feelings of shame may become involved in a religious community as a way to deny the sexual addiction and its consequences. In an attempt to become more holy, the shame-bound addict comes to the congregation to be made clean again. When a congregation is rigidly moralistic, the addict's shame increases, thus adding to his or her desire to act out in response. A congregation that is silent about sex is the perfect place in which to hide one's sex addiction. The individual can split off his or her good self from the bad self while at church. The untrained pastor or congregation will not detect the addict's ruse and may even provide the addict with a protective shelter by not seeing or naming the behavior.

When a client went to a counseling center for therapy to address the problem of her husband's sexual addiction, her pastor found out and advised her to keep the situation private, saying that he, the pastor, would advise her husband about the issue. Her pastor was neither trained in the field nor capable of addressing the whole family's responses to the addictive behavior. He actually covered up the problem and left the woman without a therapist. Too often well-intentioned lay and professional ministers venture into areas of sexual addiction and then contribute to the problem rather than healing it. By joining in an addict's denial, clergy, lay leaders, and the congregation as a whole can and do put individuals at risk.

Delusional Love Addiction

Among sexual addictions there is a condition that is sometimes called a "love addiction." Its psychiatric title is Erotomania.[8] This particular form of behavior has a delusional component. A man becomes addicted, so to speak, to the idea that someone is in love with him. A woman begins to stalk her pastor because she has, mistakenly, decided that she and her pastor can become lovers. The person with Erotomania may focus attention on same-gendered or other-gendered individuals.

The danger of this obsession is that the "love object" does not have to say or do anything to contribute to this delusion. The person with this illness selects a target love, often a religious leader, politician, or movie star. The nature of the pastoral office, with its aura of godliness, feeds and strengthens the desire of the delusional lover.

The person with Erotomania carries the delusion of "idealized romantic love and spiritual union" with someone. "Efforts to contact the object of the delusion (through telephone calls, letters, gifts, visits, and even surveillance and stalking) are common."[9] The person idealizes the relationship and feels certain that the chosen person—say, the pastor—adores him or her. Despite all boundary setting on the part of the pastor, the person holds onto the delusion that the pastor feels similarly. Few clergy or congregations are prepared to deal with this problem. A pastor who in any way sexualizes a relationship with someone like this would feed a dangerous delusion that a lasting enmeshed and obsessive relationship was possible. The person with this delusional disorder may become more and more obsessed, using verbal harassment, stalking, and even violence to gain the attention of the imagined lover.

When the Pastor Is Stalked

When I mentioned this condition at a workshop, a pastor freely disclosed that he had encountered such a person. A woman I will call Irene became active in the church following the loss of her mother. The pastor had appropriately set a few appointments with her at the office to provide grief support counseling. Toward the end of the third appointment, he tried to redirect her to a local therapist without success. She begged for and then demanded more appointment time with him.

Irene would not accept any of the boundaries that the pastor set with her. Irene, without the pastor exhibiting any behaviors to suggest this, thought that the pastor was, in fact, in love with her. When the pastor told her that this was not true and that a romantic relationship was not possible, Irene sent him a note saying that she knew they would be lovers in eternity if not in the present day. Irene was relentless in sending cards, dropping gifts off at the office, and phoning the pastor at work and home. Along with the church personnel chairperson, the pastor met with Irene and asked her to stop the behavior. They told her that she would no longer be welcome at worship or other church activities. This was a hard step for the pastor and the congregation, but the woman's behavior indicated a pervasive personality problem that was not getting better. The pastor's safety had to be protected.

A month later Irene came to the congregation in a disguise. At that point the church took legal action and a restraining order was filed against her. Church staff members were taught to screen phone calls and to delete e-mail communication from her. The pastor's phone numbers were changed. The pastor consulted with a psychologist with a specialty in this area, and this unsettling situation, we can hope, has been resolved.

I wish that I could say that this story is so rare that it will not happen in your congregation, but every clergy person is at some risk due to the nature of the crisis situations he or she deals with. Women are more at risk than men of being stalked, but as illustrated by this story, anyone can become a stalker's victim. Some surveys of healthcare professionals, psychiatrists, and other counselors indicate that as many as 53 percent of them report having been stalked.[10] Unfortunately, stalking behavior cannot be predicted on the basis of gender, class, or individual history of such behavior. The best prevention strategies include raised awareness, consultation with professionals who are experts in this area, and tending to practical matters such as the amount of personal information given out to people in the parish or community. Modifications to the office space could be made so that staff can see the door or waiting area.

You can prepare for the possibility that clergy and lay ministers in your congregation may at some time become the victims of this kind of addictive delusional behavior. When a male pastor says that a woman has become obsessed with him, this assertion must be taken seriously.

We must not assume that pastors can handle such extremely stressful situations without the help and protection of personnel committees, psychiatric consultants, and local law enforcement agencies. Thinking ahead of time about who to turn to for consultation is critical. If and when a congregational leader is stalked, the situation must be dealt with swiftly and directly. Early intervention is the best prevention in this situation.

For Personal Reflection

How do you feel when someone is paying too much attention to you? How do you let them know you're not interested? If you told someone to back off and they didn't respect your wishes, where would you turn for help?

What to Do about All This

In case you are feeling overwhelmed by the reality and dangers of sex abuse, take a deep breath. There are some practical, concrete ways to prevent a sexual abuser from using someone in your parish as his or her next victim. I will address protection issues with registered sex offenders in chapter 10, because of the unique circumstances that such issues entail. For now, I hope you will be encouraged by the next few sections on how to let everyone in your congregation know that shame, secrets, addictions, and abuse can be openly addressed to increase everyone's health and safety.

Call on Some Experts

You have some free resources to call upon to educate yourself and your congregation about these issues. My recommendation is that you contact your local child protective services agency and invite them to come to the congregation and provide workshops. They can teach you about the signs and symptoms of child abuse and neglect. The agency will also help you set clear boundaries regarding your contact with children, and will help you develop policies, like those discussed in chapters 9 and 10.

Having a workshop on child abuse will encourage people, even people who do not attend the training, to talk about the issues. The event will let abuse survivors know that you care about protection and about everyone's safety. The workshop will put potential abusers on notice that they will not be able to hide in secrecy, that you are educated about signs and symptoms, and that you will act swiftly if anything untoward takes place.

Learning to recognize the signs and symptoms of adult perpetrators is somewhat more difficult. I was recently asked to do a psychological evaluation of a teenager for the possibility of his committing an offense in the future. I turned down the request. Although there are tests that attempt to determine the likelihood of future spousal, child, or sexual abuse, none of them can actually predict the future. I told him, "I do prevention, I do intervention, but I don't do prediction." The fact that we cannot predict the future, is not however, an excuse for ignorance in the present. With intervention we can lower risk.

Prevention includes giving everyone all the information they can take in about the signs and symptoms of people in danger due to mental illness, addiction, or acute stress. Contact someone from law enforcement to provide you with education about online pornography issues for teens and adults in your community. Invite a local speaker to come and talk with your congregation about ministry to and with those who are HIV positive or living with AIDS. Inform your congregation about sexually transmitted diseases. Give teens an alternative to sexual activity, not because it is immoral but because it is holy and because there are serious emotional and physical risks in it. Enlist a local social worker or psychologist to come and talk with your congregation about mental illness and sex abuse. This information would put any past, present, or potential abusers on notice that you are using every possible resource to educate and protect the congregation.

Help to Heal the Shame

The Hebrew scriptures say, "The Lord is slow to anger, and abounding in steadfast love, forgiving iniquity and transgression, but by no means clearing the guilty, visiting the iniquity of the parents upon the children to the third and the fourth generation" (Num. 14:18). Prevention for tomorrow involves intervention and compassion toward victims today. When one child or adult is safer for having come to your congregation, you have prevented one or more generations of abuse. Your intervention is crucial.

When a person with sexual shame comes into your congregation, he or she needs to find a fellowship where lots of people are free of shame. A congregation that heals sexual shame needs unashamed leaders who talk about their own struggles with issues such as sexual harassment, sexual shame, and sexual ethics. They need to hear what the Bible has to say about issues such as incest. Sometimes such Bible passages are avoided, either by the lectionary texts or by clergy who get scared to preach about them. Texts having to do with sexual behavior need to be explored and discussed.

People need clergy and lay ministers who are clear about their own boundaries and have considered and resolved their own sexuality issues. These leaders can talk openly about the distortions of sexuality and its goodness. For example, when I offer prayers I lift up people with mental illnesses, and people with addictions to drugs, alcohol, gambling, or sex. Just adding the word *sex* to the list of addictions opens up the possibility that someone who is struggling with a sexual addiction will come to the pastor's office or call a therapist.

Sexuality needs to be affirmed as good. Its distortions need to be identified and named. When the lectionary texts recently raised the subject of bread and proclaimed Jesus as the bread of life, the true bread that satisfies, I took the opportunity to talk about hungers that satisfy and hungers that leave us lost, empty, and alone. I talked about sexual intimacy and sexual objectification. One leaves a person filled up and feeling more holy; the other leaves one feeling shame.

When I ask clergy to talk about these things, I do not minimize the risk I am asking them to take. When I recently prepared to preach on the subject of incest in King David's family (2 Samuel 13), I was not sure what feedback I might get. I found myself so scared early on Sunday morning that I called my sister to tell her I wanted to back out of it and use an old sermon from the barrel. She let me know that this would be okay, of course, but once I knew that she would be praying for me, I found courage and went ahead with it.

After the sermon I was still a bit shaky and wondered what people would say to me as they went through the line. One woman said, "The subject of sex abuse is so complicated, we need someone to talk about it with us. I thank you." A man began to speak to me and became overwhelmed with tears. "Thank you" was all that I could actually make out from his tear-choked words. While I went into the pulpit that morning with my parents' voices in my head, saying, "You shouldn't talk about that!" I also knew that the sermon held the potential for healing. Some members of the congregation would possibly commit themselves to discussing the secrets and abuses that have wounded them. This could be the beginning of their healing. People need courageous pastoral leadership when it comes to issues of sexual shame.

Shame is uniquely healed by grace, which Christian faith unabashedly proclaims. While guilt says "I messed up," and I can change and be forgiven, shame says "I *am* messed up" and requires doses of grace to be healed. In the inner core of our souls, we all hunger for acceptance—a feeling that people with sexual shame rarely experience. A person with a good deal of sexual shame is a person in search of redemption. Shame is the underlying spiritual malaise that hovers around the person who has been violated or has violated sexual boundaries. This person is likely to search out a seat in the sanctuary in order to be healed. Mental health treatment and behavior modification are effective in treating all aspects of sexual abuse: addiction, behavior, and its aftermath. (Grace is the only antidote to shame.)

Finally, clergy and laity alike need to create congregations that are full of grace. If you are like me, you need a fellowship where your particular sins do not make you less worthy than people with a different sins. I need a place where my past is acknowledged, where I have the opportunity to heal in the present, where I can speak the truth in love. I want to worship where I am protected from harm, where the harms that have befallen me do not remain stuck on me like cooties. I need a place of grace, where "you are my beloved" is the weekly call to worship. We can create those places.

SEVEN

Clergy at Risk

As many as one-third of clergy are at risk of crossing a sexual boundary at some time in their career, and the risk for sexual misconduct goes up with the number of years of service. Now is the time for a careful analysis of the contributing factors. In this chapter I review a number of cultural, psychological, and congregational factors that put clergy at particular risk for sexual misconduct. They include cultural factors, such as the discrediting of the role of clergy in literature and the popular press, and gender-bound stereotypes about vocational roles. They include psychological factors of particular concern to clergy, including depression and vocational disenchantment. The risk of clergy crossing a sexual boundary includes congregational factors such as enmeshment, codependency, and on-the-job burnout. We begin by opening the pages of an old, old story with a freshly familiar modern sound.

Cultural Factors

Two prevailing cultural factors put clergy at risk. The first is the reality that clergy were once among the most esteemed professionals in both Eastern and Western culture. In Northern Laos, for example, the king is viewed as the most powerful person in the society, closely followed by the shaman, and then teachers. In North American parishes the pastor's level of authority and honor has been declining in the past few decades. Pastors were once viewed as community leaders and fully involved in civic and fraternal organizations. In my first parish, I was called upon to give the invocation at the Moose Lodge, a job previously held by all of the male pastors of that congregation. To their credit the lodge members invited me to attend and to stand among the male leadership of the community. I stood beneath a large stuffed moose head and invoked the spirit of the Most High God, feeling as if I was a tribal elder myself.

Clergy have been losing these roles as community and civic leaders. There are many reasons for this, but high among them is the issue of clergy sexual conduct and the media's hyperfocus on fallen saints. The much publicized erosion of clergy integrity affects clergy esteem and effectiveness in building community partnerships and exercising political leverage to serve the poor and homeless. In a recent gathering of clergy, a colleague remarked that we are a profession of the embarrassing and the embarrassed.

A second cultural factor at work in every congregation is the changing roles of men and women in society. When women were first ordained in many mainline Protestant traditions, there was a good deal of talk about the feared feminization of the role of pastor. Theologians took pen to paper to describe Jesus and his masculine attributes. (The feminization of Jesus was also feared.) Clergymen, who had once seen themselves as male professionals among other male professionals, began to see their roles changing. As the pastoral roles of nurturer and caretaker, shepherd and healer came to the foreground, images of the pastor as civic leader were fading.

Both men and women experience gender discrimination in the parish—women for being in a male profession, and oddly enough, men for being in the feminine role of nurturing and educating the flock. Let's explore more about these dynamics and ways that changing cultural images of clergy could lead to clergy and lay ministers crossing sexual boundaries.

The Public Image

The once-esteemed roles of pastor, priest, and rabbi have been losing public respect. When Nathaniel Hawthorne's novel *The Scarlet Letter* appeared in 1850, it began a trend in literature describing the fall of clergy to the sin of sexual desire. In the story, the Reverend Dimmesdale falls in love with a young married woman named Hester Prynne, and they have a secretive affair. When she becomes pregnant, she is shamed by the community and forced to wear a scarlet *A* (for adulteress) on her chest wherever she goes. The Reverend Dimmesdale never confesses to the congregation or the community. He tells Hester:

> It was my folly! I have said it. But, up to that epoch of my life, I had lived in vain. The world had been so cheerless! My heart was a habitation large enough for many guests, but lonely and chill and without a household fire. . . . And so, Hester, I drew thee into my heart, into its innermost chamber, and sought to warm thee by the warmth which thy presence made there![1]

The book so fascinated readers that it has remained a classic. In the latest movie version, the authors of the screenplay were so smitten by the lusty love of its main characters that they changed the ending and had the Reverend Dimmesdale and Hester run off together to live happily ever after.

The culture has been fascinated by clergy who seduce or are seduced by women. In the 1970s, a novel was turned into a television series, *The Thorn Birds,* with Richard Chamberlain as its romantic leading man. This mini-series focused on a love affair between a priest and a parishioner. The priest became the fantasy love of many American women, while at the same time conveying a message that a clergyman's sexual desires are his undoing. The moral integrity of the office of priest or pastor eroded from the first to the last episode.

The media continue to make stories such as these into melodramas, rather than describing the very real tension between the desire for "forbidden" passion and the supposed opposite, the upright life—a tension experienced by both clergy and their lovers. Lacking in media and literature are images of clergy who are both deeply passionate and who have moral integrity. Religious tradition and the media have disseminated a belief that clergy must choose between sexual passion and ethical behavior. This gulf between passion and ethics results in either dispassionate religious leaders who are ethical, or unethical leaders who defy convention with their lusty sexuality. This gap has left clergy confused, disembodied, and yet tempted, even thrilled, to take romantic and sexual risks.

Public interest in the sex lives of clergy continues to grow. It could be argued that there is no more sexual misconduct taking place today than 150 years ago, that there is only more public exposure of the misconduct. Across denominations roughly 30 percent of clergy anonymously report having crossed a sexual boundary and engaged in sexual intimacy with someone in their parish.[2] This level of sexual harassment and abuse has been acknowledged in anonymous surveys, but only recently acknowledged within the profession itself.

Secrecy and silence on the issue of sexual abuse in the church has meant that growing numbers of laity have turned to the law and to the media to plead their cases. Some of this publicity has increased one of the root causes of the abuse itself—shaming and discrediting the profession. Where once clergy automatically held respect, favor, and political power, they now find themselves suspect. They are no longer seen, nor see themselves, as the ethical standard barriers.

Clergy are satirized in late-night comedy and are the subjects of scandalous headlines on the front pages of major newspapers across the nation. When reporters interview judicatory leaders and bishops, these leaders often appear (or are portrayed as) ignorant, callous toward victims, and self-serving protectors of the institution of the church.

The decline in the respect for the vocation itself is evident among seminary recruiters. Fewer people are choosing the vocation. Seminaries are laying off staff and finding that the majority of new recruits are those in midlife career change. Fewer first-career individuals enter seminary to join a profession that no longer holds great dignity and whose salaries reflect a decline in prestige.

These stories affect clergy vocational esteem and increase our fear that we will become like them or that we are already ignorant, callous, and self-serving. There is a good deal of shame among clergy for the role and vocation itself. The experience of another fallen colleague leaves pastors more isolated and lonely in their grief and sometimes wondering if an old boundary-crossing or former sexualized relationship may reappear to ruin their careers. "Am I next?" is a common phrase, particularly among male clergy who even with clear consciences about past behaviors realize that none of us is fully protected against false accusations. Under this cloud of fear and suspicion, pastoral leadership declines and clergy may become withdrawn, irritable, or controlling. Each person responds to the silent fear of suspicion differently. Clergy often feel isolated and discouraged as they attempt to correct institutional neglect in handling sexual boundary issues that have arisen in the past few decades.

> ***For Personal Reflection***
>
> How do films and television programs portray clergy? What qualities do the fictitious clergy possess? What qualities do clergy you know possess? How have the media portrayals or public scandals changed your view of clergy whom you know personally?

Gender, Bias, and Role Expectations

When we examine why clergy no longer enjoy the high esteem they once did, we can identify a wide array of factors. The first way we looked at this issue was through the eyes of literature and media. The second cultural factor is changing gender roles and the odd reality that both male and female clergy are maligned for being in the wrong gender role. Being discredited for crossing perceived gender roles may undermine a clergy person's self-esteem and contribute to sexual misconduct. A clergy person may seek to restore his or her sense of gender role (femininity or masculinity) through romantic sexual encounters.

In the United States, the dominant culture tends to define gender rather rigidly. A person is understood to be either male or female, and certain behaviors and roles are expected of each. While these roles and expectations have been changing, especially in the past two decades, some of their vestiges remain. The interesting reality about the vocation of pastoral ministry is that this is a job that includes both masculine and feminine gender constructs, culturally shaped norms expected of each gender.

A pastor provides exhortation, chairs a meeting, organizes a budget, launches a building project, manages and supervises staff. These have traditionally been male roles. A pastor also provides spiritual counseling, guidance, and moral support; looks after the needs of children; and feeds the poor. These have been traditionally female roles. What has that meant for clergy? It has meant that women pastors are criticized for exercising leadership and preaching, if they are too pushy or tend to take charge. Male pastors receive criticism for being soft or henpecked by the women of the church. A person with a damaged sense of masculinity or femininity might engage in sexual affairs in an attempt to restore a sense of gender identity. The erosion of gender integrity can lead clergy into sexualized relationships in misguided attempts to restore a sense of "right" gender.

Not all cultures view gender or spiritual leadership in this way, however. In the Native American tradition the most revered leaders of the community are called "two-spirits," also known as the *berdache.* Anthropologists have found these spiritual leaders in many different native tribes. They were considered to be two genders at the same time, that is, two-spirits. They were highly valued and selected through the interpretation of their dreams. A dream may also tell the two-spirit to relinquish the honor and to return to his or her former gender. The *berdache* has ability to understand the world from beyond the narrow experience or viewpoint of only one gender.

The concept of a gender-free holy person is mind-expanding for those of us who have been raised in a tradition with rigid gender expectations. It is an unsettling experience to be uncertain of one's role and the gender expectations of it. The two-spirit concept provides an interesting and shame-free model for clergy who are stuck between the poles of rigid gender constructs. Although we are admittedly far from viewing our religious leaders as people who are two-spirits, clergy could begin to see themselves in this way, embracing the multifaceted gender roles within the profession.

One pastor described his feelings to me in this way. "I don't feel like a man in this job. I'm doing so many things that women usually do, like running the Sunday school, sitting at the hospital with the sick, handholding nervous volunteers." He described stress in the vocation as the erosion of his sense of masculinity. He remarked, "It's not a good time to be male. I'm supposed to feel bad about myself if I want to have more power, be more assertive, demand to be respected." This man had entered into an affair with a key lay leader. With her, he felt that someone not only recognized his masculinity but also desired him for it. For this man, the impotence he felt within the profession contributed to low self-esteem, which in turn contributed to his seeking the ego boost of an affair.

Limiting gender roles also place clergywomen at risk. Clergywomen face job discrimination in multiple ways. Congregations have seen their women pastors in the "mothering" role and resented them for taking time off to mother their own children. Rather than rejoicing in the dual roles of parent and professional, clergywomen may become pulled and stretched between competing demands. Conversely, they may be accepted as pastoral caregivers but resented when they take the role of leader or manager, roles that have been more traditionally masculine. Women experience real internal and external pressure to be exceptionally good at what they do to show that they are competent on the job. This pressure leads to overwork, codependency, and acute levels of burnout.

Congregations have discriminated against clergywomen in patterns that are similar to discrimination against women in other professional vocations. So-called glass ceilings have been evident when congregations do not even consider women for senior pastor in a multiple-staff setting. Wage discrimination has been prevalent. A church was recently hiring a new pastor. Their previous pastor had been working part time in the church and part time as a substitute teacher to keep the small congregation running. When the time for a change came up, both the outgoing pastor and an elder told me, "We'll have to hire a woman if we want to get someone full time. No men would take the job at the pay we can offer."

Blatant gender discrimination is rampant. A clergywoman in the associate pastor role in her congregation recently asked for a raise and was told by the senior pastor, "Other women in our denomination make a lot less than the men, and many of them don't even find jobs." In other words, "You should be happy that you have a job at all." A priest named Rhonda was repeatedly denied raises. The church's governing board told her that since her husband had a job, she was the "second wage earner" in the family and the amount that she made was insignificant. These attitudes have led to spiritual and psychological challenges for clergywomen.

Gender-directed harassment is described as a serious impediment to ministry by two-thirds of all clergywomen. Most of these women feel extremely vulnerable in situations of harassment. Feeling already discredited for choosing a male vocation, they fear that if they report these incidents, they will be seen as even less creditable victims and be resented for having spoken up against a person of greater power or esteem. From a young age, women are taught to believe that they will be disbelieved when they speak up about sexual abuse. They are also taught that it is their fault if it happens. On the other hand, if a woman is the perpetrator of a boundary crossing, she probably keeps silent, believing that she will be more swiftly and unjustly dismissed than one of her more esteemed male colleagues. Whether perpetrator or victim, she chooses silence as the best of her bad options. While she keeps silence, her work erodes, her relational competence declines, she may be cognitively distracted or confused, and she may suffer from an acute stress disorder, or become chronically depressed.

Clearly, role expectations and assumptions based on gender limit clergy of both genders and put clergy and congregations at risk.

> *For Personal Reflection*
>
> How has your pastor (or how have you as a pastor) been limited by or criticized by gender bias? With whom have you spoken about it? What could the congregation do to examine the possibility of gender bias and to address inequalities?

Congregational Factors

Two dynamics in congregational leadership hold great potential to erode a pastor's wellness. The first is *enmeshment*, particularly expressed as the expectation that a pastor's entire life will be spent within the congregation. The second and related dynamic is that of *codependency*, which is fostered by a clergy person's family of origin issues and by the vocation itself. These two dynamics lead to clergy boundary violations and full-blown clergy sexual misconduct.

The Pastoral Role and Enmeshment

The American Heritage Dictionary defines *enmeshment* as "to entangle, as if in a mesh." *Enmeshment* is a psychological condition in which one is caught in a mesh of relationships from which one cannot escape. When in enmeshed relationships, a person's growth and maturity are limited and individual identity is diminished. The true self gives way to a false self who tries to fit the role of perfect family member. An enmeshed family system co-opts the individual's true identity. Enmeshed individuals feel that their identity is almost indistinguishable from others in the emotional system.

Pastoral leaders suffer from enmeshed relationships with their congregations. This may be due to the pastor's unfinished issues from his or her family of origin. It may be due to the congregation's lack of maturity and intolerance for individual differences. If the pastor and congregation are both predisposed to enmeshment, both will be stifled and individual and corporate growth will be extremely limited.

It is common for a pastor and congregation to become enmeshed. The vocation of pastoral ministry has been established and maintained on the assumption that the pastor can and will give all of his or her life to Christ and that this commitment will be demonstrated by giving unending hours of service to a congregation to which he or she is called. The congregation interprets the pastor's call to serve to mean that he or she will give every minute of thought and activity to the congregation. There is an expectation of enmeshment—that the pastors and congregants will all be close to each other and that all of them will be loyal to the congregation at the expense of individual growth and individuation.

What behaviors are characteristic of enmeshed congregational systems? Parishioners resent clergy taking time off or involvement in community activities. Clergy who give all of their time and efforts to their congregations, even to the point of family neglect or emotional exhaustion, are rewarded and reinforced by praise, promotion, and peer admiration.

In my first parish the personnel committee asked me for an accounting of my work hours. I listed every activity for a month. When it came time to discuss the hours, I was surprised to find that the committee began taking things off the list. First, they said the church camping trip was family time for me and not work time. I was shocked. How could I *not* have gone? How could I explain to them that church events are all work events to me? The situation grew worse. They took coffee hour off the list. This, they said, was social time, not work time. My discomfort was turning to rage. Would they have accepted it if I'd gone home after the last handshake in the receiving line? This conversation was, for me, a culture shock. I was learning about their expectations. I found myself sulking about having to give my free time away and having to put in hours at the office that the committee thought were volunteer hours and social fun. Their excuse for disrespecting my individual time and dishonoring my work time was that this was a small town, and everyone knew everyone's business anyway. I was, in effect, expected to have multiple relationship roles, to lose my privacy, and to enmesh with the church family.

Pastors who do not take time off to be alone or engage in friendships outside of the congregation are in danger of getting their emotional and intimacy needs met within the congregation, too. The enmeshed congregational system has the same emotional qualities as an incestuous family. When people become too close to one another and the boundaries between individuals are blurred, the stage is set for abuse. These blurred emotional boundaries lead to the blurring of other boundaries, creating a sense that one can develop any kind of relationship (even a sexual one) within the system, and it will be all right. A clergy person in a system that encourages unending church activity and emotional attachment as part and parcel of the job may try to meet all of his or her intimacy needs inside the congregational system.

Clergy are pressured by congregations and denominational leaders to be enmeshed with their congregations. Twenty years ago I witnessed the fight in the United Methodist Church to change the definition of ministry to include part-time work in pastoral ministry. Many colleagues could not even imagine part-time work as ministry. Young clergy who were planning for families pushed the issue through in the face of a great deal of hostile resentment. There is still suspicion about anyone who serves in less than full-time ministry. A few years ago a bishop told the gathering of clergy that he considered full-time service in the church to be 80 hours a week. Anything less than that was a source of shame. This cultural reality in most denominations has played a role in the burnout and depressive symptoms of clergy and in the incidence of sexual misconduct.

Prolonged work and the prolonged stress that accompanies work in a closed system create physical and mental illness. Without sufficient time outside of the church family for recreation, intimacy with a partner, and other restorative activities, clergy suffer. If one's work becomes all consuming, then an energy-raising, titillating affair, a fanaticized or real lover, or a new sexual experience provides an escape. In an enmeshed system, warning sirens about the dangers of these liaisons do not sound.

> *For Personal Reflection*
>
> When have you felt enmeshed in your family, church, or workplace? When have you felt that you were expected to devote all of your time and energy to a person or group?

The Honored Codependent

In family systems study, the dynamics of enmeshment and codependency are similar, in that both enmeshed and codependent clergy protect the church family system by self-sacrifice. Clergy in both roles are likely to become stressed, overtired, and anxious in ministry. The dynamics are different in that an enmeshed pastor will give up his or her happiness in order to stay in the family system, while the codependent pastor will give up happiness to fix the system.

The term *codependent* was first used to characterize individuals who supported alcoholics by tolerating and even enabling their addictions. The codependent covers up problems, and finds ways to disseminate information that keeps the family looking good to outsiders. The codependent runs interference with members of the family who would otherwise expose the alcoholic. The codependent, we could say, becomes addicted to the addict. The role of helping and fixing becomes primary. For example, an alcoholic's husband will support his wife's drinking by ignoring it, purchasing alcohol for her, or telling her doctor that her recent fall was the result of inattention, rather than her drunken stupor.

Children in these families learn the role of helper and give up their own desires, goals, and happiness to fix the situation. The child becomes convinced that the family can be fixed with enough of the child's love, enough self-sacrifice, enough of whatever he or she believes is lacking in the family system. This child often carries these feelings into adult relationships and work life.

Many clergy are codependent. The pastor may or may not have learned the codependent role in the family of origin. Overwork and a lack of personal boundaries, obliviousness to one's own needs, and a desire to save others at all costs permeates the ministry of the codependent individual.

Some congregations are addictive organizations, functioning in ways that are out of control and negative. Pastors may become codependent in such congregations, trying to fix the congregation and believing that they have the power to do so. Codependent clergy try to rescue a congregation that is stuck in real or imagined dysfunction. Rather than take additional time off to cope with a high stress job, the codependent pastor will work even harder. We could say that this pastor becomes addicted to the congregation. Ann Wilson Schaef and Diane Fassel, in their book *The Addictive Organization,* describe an addiction, saying, "If there is something we are not willing to give up in order to make our lives fuller and more healthy, it probably can be classified as an addiction."[3]

Congregations rejoice in, honor, and reward the unhealthy pastor's martyrdom, as illustrated by the bishop's comment that pastors are supposed to work 80 hours per week. Congregations expect pastors to practically live at their churches. (With parsonages next door to churches, many of them do.) Overworked clergy are rewarded with praise, and those who ask for time off are often shamed and resented for it. The ultimate example of this sacrificial life is no less than Christ's death on the cross. Christ's martyrdom is used to reinforce the pastor's supposed salvific role. The codependent pastor will turn to the symbol of Christ, whose very life was given for the salvation of the flock. Not only is this bad theology (Jesus was the complete and last victim required for the sake of the world's salvation), but it results in exhausted and anxious clergy.

What happens to the pastor as a result of constant and unrelenting stress? The adrenaline system ceases to function in its usual healthy way to handle stress. The immune system is weakened and the body more open to infection. The brain seeks highs and the person turns to alcohol, drugs, or sexual stimulation. High levels of stress cause wise people to make poor choices, due to mental confusion. They end up doing things that they ordinarily would not do.

Many a sexual boundary crossing has been confessed with the explanation, "I just lost my mind." While this is no legitimate excuse, it rightly explains the way prolonged stress, martyrdom, and the fatigue of endless effort can affect judgment. In order to make sound decisions at a moment of sexual opportunity or seduction, a pastor must be rested, spiritually grounded, and in good physical and mental health.

For Personal Reflection

What situations in family or congregation have you tried to fix or save? How were your attempts rewarded or rebuffed? How do you stay objective about your involvement in the problems of your congregation? What do you do for self-care?

Congregations need to stop fostering unhealthy behavior patterns in their pastors and instead reward them for time off, physical fitness, playful times with friends and family, and spiritual renewal. Ending patterns of enmeshment and codependency involves a change in the whole system to support clergy self-care. Neither clergy nor laity can exhaust themselves out of a sense of duty or obligation without becoming spiritually and emotionally drained. No one can fix a congregation's problems by self-sacrifice. Inevitably, others will be sacrificed, too.

EIGHT

Dangers in Pastoral Counseling

As clergy fulfill their call to service in the church they participate in joyful events such as births and marriages, and painful events such as the loss of a job, relocation to a new community, divorce, and death. Clergy often receive the first call from a family in need of crisis support, such as intervention with a loved one who is mentally ill, or at the scene of an accident. Clergy who serve as counselors particularly enter into the intimate stories of members of their congregation and community. Some clergy fill nearly half of their work week with counseling.

Congregations are at risk when a pastor enters a counseling relationship with a parishioner, whether a child, adolescent, or adult. When a pastor serves in the counseling role there is a significant chance that relationships will deepen and become psychologically and emotionally intimate. This can lead a parishioner to develop a deepening trust in the pastor's counseling competence, even in situations where the pastor is incompetent. As the counseling relationship and trust deepens further, the pastor or the person receiving the care may begin to feel that this level of intimacy is romantic or sexual. Since romantic relationships between clergy and parishioners violate ethical principles and sexual harassment policies, this level of intimacy can put either or both of them at risk.

Congregations are at risk when their pastors provide counseling because most clergy lack the training, supervision, and continuing education necessary for handling complex sexual and mental health issues. Clergy serving as parish counselors are frequently working beyond their level of training. Ethical counseling demands that providers be in counseling or under supervision themselves at all times. This protects them from engaging in a person's problems in such a way that it is unhealthy and stressful for them. Pastors of local congregations who provide counseling without adequate training are dangerous to themselves and others.

The counseling role places clergy at risk for other reasons, as well. Clergy often serve as crisis counselors. In this role they are likely to experience secondary trauma and trauma bonding. These conditions arise in the midst of a sudden and presumably one-time situation, but they can last for months beyond the initial crisis. After prolonged involvement with crisis situations, pastors may not even be aware of subsequent damage to their own mental health. Before long they have depleted their inner resources.

Even apart from the risks inherent in crisis counseling, those who give of themselves in this most intimate of roles can end up carrying the stress of the congregation in isolation. Depression can overwhelm the helping professional at any time and may be expressed overtly through the crossing of boundaries or covertly through addictions. Depression is also closely linked with vocational burnout. The depressed pastor may become overwhelmed and express a desire to leave the vocation altogether or cross a sexual boundary as a way to escape the prolonged stress of the vocation passively.

Training and Continuing Education

As I have suggested, many issues arise in counseling situations that most clergy are not trained to address. One or two courses in general counseling may be provided in seminary education, but too few classes teach clergy how to recognize individuals with chronic or severe mental illnesses. Most are not trained in the recognition of personality disorders, crisis intervention theories and techniques, post-traumatic stress response, or medical conditions that lead to mental health problems. Most have only broad knowledge of issues such as family violence, child sex abuse, addictions, and marital conflict but have not had specific training in healing interventions.

Seminaries include overview courses on counseling and the practice of pastoral care. They provide courses in ethics, such as boundary setting in the pastoral relationship. This may be the full extent of a local pastor's training. There are clergy who study counseling professionally and who become members of the American Association of Pastoral Counselors. These clergy have extensive training and supervision and are often state-licensed counseling professionals. Licensed counselors are required by their licensure boards to have undertaken 3,000 to 5,000 hours of supervised counseling during their training and internships. They are also required to take between 15 and 25 hours of ongoing training each year in order to remain licensed. They have accountability and are excellent resources for local congregations.

Clergy are at greater risk in the counseling relationship when they lack professional training, licensure, or standing in an accredited counseling program. Local pastors are not like other professional counselors. Generally clergy do not have specific codes of ethics to guide their work, or hours of supervision. Local church pastors are generally not required to obtain any updated ethical training or education in other aspects of their professional work. They are not required to obtain supervision, and too few of them initiate supervision on their own.

Professional counselors are trained extensively in sexual ethics, including how to handle individuals in counseling who express a romantic or sexual attraction, and are required to take annual coursework in child abuse. But clergy usually lack this training and might even resist it. When the clergy of the United Methodist churches in the West were required by their bishops to take training on sexual ethics and sexual abuse, many of them were vocally resistant. This was the first time that any of them could remember having been required to engage in education since seminary.

It is no wonder then that clergy both consciously and in ignorance blunder into sexualized relationships with those they counsel. Wise congregations require their pastors and lay staff to take training at local offices of child protective services and to take ethics courses offered by local counselors. Clergy who counsel without regular supervision under the leadership of trained therapists are at risk and are putting their congregations at risk.

Scope of Practice

Some pastors are trained pastoral counselors, and then there are pastors who think they are counselors. The second of these two groups is more at risk of becoming engaged in sexually abusive behavior. Three crucial ethical issues for clergy are whether or not they actually counsel people in the parish, whom they choose to counsel, and the duration of the counseling relationship. These issues are elements of what is called the scope of practice.

A person who has no training in marital therapy should not try to counsel a couple in conflict. For example, couples therapists are trained to determine whether there is domestic violence within the relationship. New counseling theories suggest that couples therapy is damaging and inappropriate in situations where one partner uses power and dominance to gain compliance. If the woman is being verbally or physically abused, anything she says in the counseling session can be used by her husband to further blame or abuse her at home. The counselor refuses to see the husband and wife together until the issue of equality and safety can be addressed. Too often, well-meaning clergy intervene in situations where they could do more harm than good, largely because they are natural helpers. The pastor needs to consider the level of training and expertise he or she has in every area before embarking on counseling relationships. Referral to local therapists is often the best idea.

Pastors who are not trained counselors may tend to share too much of their personal lives with parishioners, setting the stage for what may be interpreted as friendship or romance. Some pastors want to be more of a friend to parishioners than a professional. When a pastor expresses this sentiment it means that the pastor is trying to get his or her needs for intimacy met through contact with parishioners. When the pastor conveys an attitude that "we are in this together," it could be that a relationship is forming that is no longer just a counseling relationship. The professional role is different from the relationship of friendship. A professional's job is to meet the needs of the parishioner and to leave his or her own needs out of the relationship entirely.

The pastor who counsels parishioners cannot be effective unless he or she remains objective. The role of counselor becomes quite complex when the pastor has prior knowledge of an individual or family when one of them comes into the office for counseling. For example, a young woman comes to her pastor's office to seek counsel about her relationship with a young man in the congregation whom she is dating. The pastor knows from conversations with the young man's family that he has a drug problem. What will the pastor do? Can the pastor maintain objective concern for the young woman? Does the pastor hold back confidential information or share it with the woman? The pastor, by having many relationships with people in the same system, has regular dilemmas about the confidentiality of information known and shared.

Specific training in issues of counseling ethics, transference in the counseling relationship, and handling sexual issues ought to be required for every pastor. Those who meet with parishioners more than one or two times need to have additional training. Clergy who go through crises with parish families need to consult a peer professional to be sure that he or she is handling the situation appropriately. Personnel committees and pastors should engage in frank conversations about the amount of counseling work of the pastor, his or her sources of training, and a plan for ongoing supervision. Congregations can also assist their pastors by sending them to workshops for counselors to increase their skill in handling complicated relationships, sexual issues in pastoral counseling, and crisis intervention.

For Personal Reflection

List various situations for which a pastor might be called upon for counseling. How can members of congregations encourage clergy in setting limits, knowing when he or she is in too deep, and in making referrals?

Secondary Trauma

In addition to lack of extensive training and supervision in the high-risk field of pastoral counseling, clergy can be at greater risk of entering into sexualized relationships when they have been through a traumatic event or series of events with parishioners. The pastor's intimate involvement with people in times of acute illness, bereavement, sudden loss, natural disasters, and other times of crisis can be stressful. As noted earlier, prolonged stress depletes energy and affects moods. Multiple situations or even just a few situations involving acute stress may result in the helper being affected by the trauma as well.

I recall a time in my own pastoral ministry when I had a funeral every week for six weeks. At the end of that time, I pressed on as if I were immune to the experience. I was unaware that what was happening to me had a name or that the symptoms I was experiencing—irritability, fatigue, heart palpitations, appetite loss, and sleeplessness—are symptoms of secondary trauma.

The terms *secondary trauma* and *vicarious trauma* are used by psychologists to describe the helper's response to a traumatic experience that he or she witnesses secondarily. For example, after September 11, 2001, psychologists, pastors, and Red Cross workers who had flown into New York from all over the country found themselves experiencing stress symptoms similar to those of the people they helped. They felt restless, overwhelmed with emotions, unable to concentrate, and prone to tears. They were vulnerable to the pain of others. Clergy who were there and clergy who buried victims of this tragedy became aware of their own need for psychological help in the months following September 11. Congregations can assist clergy who serve as crisis counselors by providing funding for them to receive consultation and psychological counseling in the weeks following the traumatic event.

Trauma Bonding

Clergy are also often among the first people at the scene of a tragedy. In such cases, they experience their own traumatic responses and face subsequent symptoms. In addition to experiencing psychological symptoms from secondary trauma, people who go through traumatic circumstances can be unusually drawn together in what is known as trauma bonding. A pastor and parishioner brought together by trauma can experience this phenomenon.

Mike was the pastor of a new suburban church. A young couple arrived in the community. They were quite enthusiastically in love, having just met each other and married quickly after two months in treatment for alcohol and drug abuse. They were friends in recovery from their addictions yet far from emotionally healed. The wife, Meilie, was addressing her underlying issues in therapy and asked the pastor to provide spiritual counseling and offer prayer with her. One afternoon,

Pastor Mike received an urgent call from the sheriff's office that Meilie had come home and found her husband dead of a self-inflicted gunshot wound. The sheriff asked Mike to come to the house and be with her.

Mike left his desk in disarray and went. With his best pastoral skills, he supported her and kept his focus on her. But Mike had no training in trauma work. He had never seen a violent crime scene. He was churning internally and excused himself to the bathroom to vomit. He knew that if the scene was this hard for him, it might not be the best for her to stay in the house and assisted her in going to the local hospital for medications and a night of sleep. Mike went back to the office. (Yes, back to the office!) He just pushed on through the day, as if it were an ordinary day.

That night he did not sleep. He spent the night clinging to his wife, but he did not tell her much about the incident. Even though he was profoundly shaken by the experience, he kept thinking he would get over it. He did not take any time off, because his parishioners always complained when he did that. He felt guilty when he left them for even one day, let alone the few days that he needed. He minimized his own pain from the trauma he had seen.

People in the parish heard about the situation and noticed that Mike seemed really sad on Sunday. His sermon was poorly organized, and he delivered it without energy, but they did not say anything to him. They, too, thought he would just get over it.

Mike, like many clergy, did not have a counselor or a colleague he could talk to about the situation. He was embarrassed that it was bothering him and thought he should be man enough to handle it. So he kept on going to work. He also regularly met with and counseled Meilie in order to help her through this traumatic time in her life. He even increased his time with her to twice a week. Before long he found himself looking forward to her visits. He took extra time to groom himself on those days. He chose clothes that would help him to feel handsome. The two of them talked about the situation and relived it in the hope of getting rid of the terrible memories they had of it.

What Mike was experiencing with Meilie is called trauma bonding. Two people, having experienced a similar trauma, have a secret understanding of the event and the emotions surrounding it. Although he could not seem to explain the horror he felt about the scene to his wife, he did not have to explain with Meilie. It did not take long for him to feel as if he were deeply in love with her. He believed that she deserved a better life and his healing touch.

Trauma can be dangerous if it is not handled appropriately. Mike needed to seek counseling for himself within a few days of the initial shock. He needed his parishioners to tell him, even demand, that he take time away from the parish. They could have scheduled a preacher for the next Sunday and given him and his wife a gift certificate to a hotel on the coast. They could have told him that they were seeing signs of his stress and worked with him to develop a plan of self-care.

Mike needed to trust Meilie's therapist to work with her about her own traumatic responses. He also could have referred Meilie to another pastor in the area while he took time to get away, become more objective, and deal with his attraction toward her. He could then have redirected her for pastoral counseling to the other pastor and limited his time with her to Sunday worship. Any of these steps would have reduced his vulnerability and increased his ability to use wisdom and good judgment.

For Personal Reflection

When have you experienced trauma? Were other people involved in the situation? Did your relationship with them change, and if so, how? What have been your feelings toward the people who went through it with you since then?

Multiple Relationships

In this situation, Mike and Meilie had two relationships. One relationship was that of pastor and parishioner. The second relationship was shaped by the trauma experience. A professional who has two different role relationships with someone has what is known as a dual or multiple relationship.

For example, a pastor who chooses friends from among parishioners ends up having two relationships with them. In one, the pastor has power and authority and is the one in the helping role. In the other, the pastor is in a mutually beneficial friendship. While a pastor would not likely disclose personal problems with a parishioner, the pastor would likely disclose those problems with a friend. Being in those two roles simultaneously is complicated and can lead to the crossing of other boundaries. When a personal relationship is combined with a pastoral relationship, the amount of time the people spend together increases and the amount of personal disclosure increases. These friendships may be viewed by one or both people as romantic.

A multiple relationship would also occur if a pastor hires a woman from the congregation as a housekeeper. In this case the pastor has two relationships with the person: boss and spiritual leader. The housekeeper would also gain more personal knowledge of the pastor than other parishioners have, setting the stage for her to think of herself as special and to imagine a more intimate relationship.

The term *multiple relationships* was first used in the counseling field to describe the problems that arise when a counselor has two or more relationships with a client. Therapists are trained to avoid such relationships. For example, a counselor would not counsel a person who is a social friend. A counselor would not join a client at a baseball game. A psychologist would not counsel a student from a class that he or she was teaching. These are considered to be unethical situations, because having two or more types of relationships with clients distorts the objectivity necessary for the professional relationship.

Clergy who are in the counseling role have many multiple relationships. A pastor counseled a woman about a problem in her marriage on Tuesday, and on Saturday night sat next to her and her estranged husband at a church social. He felt awkward throughout the event. When jokes went around the table, he was surprised to find himself telling one about an estranged wife. This compromised his professional role. Another pastor was invited to a pool party to celebrate her ministry, and she sat in a hot tub next to her lay leader. When he began to flirt with her—standard social hot tub behavior—she could not figure out how to deal with this professionally. If she had gone to the event in her work clothes, or even suggested that the event be held in a banquet room or the church social hall, she would have avoided this dilemma.

As noted earlier, there is an expectation within most congregations that the pastor will have multiple relationships with members. This makes it difficult to notice the subtle problems that are created by a pastor simultaneously having several kinds of relationships with a parishioner. Multiple relationships have been seen as normal, and in this normalcy, the pitfalls are overlooked. It is especially wise for a pastor who is counseling a parishioner to keep a professional distance from that person in fellowship settings, so that conversations do not reveal anything about the confidences that have been shared in the pastoral counseling office.

Has the pastor become more personal with one or more parishioners than would be acceptable, say, in a relationship between a doctor and patient, or counselor and patient? It is vital that each pastor explore personal boundaries about relationships in the parish, motivations for multiple relationships, and the complications that such relationships create. The clergy person also needs to articulate those boundaries with the personnel committee and enlist committee members' help in interpreting clergy behavior to the congregation.

For Personal Reflection

Review the list of guidelines for maintaining professional boundaries at the end of this chapter. How would you modify it to fit your congregation? How could use make use of this tool for the clergy and laity of your congregation?

Depression and Burnout

While clergy could fall victim to any one of a number of psychological conditions, two seem particularly prevalent among clergy who cross over sexual boundaries. The first is depression. As many as one in three people suffers from depression at some time in life. Some of the causes of depression are unresolved grief experiences, traumatic experiences, and prolonged stress at home or on the job. Depression can be the underlying condition of many addictive behaviors, including sex or love addiction. The depressed person is more vulnerable to sexual affairs.

The second condition is that of vocational crisis, including burnout, a loss of commitment to a previously chosen career, and a sense that one's ideals and the reality do not match in the chosen vocation. Studies have shown that the longer a person is in a counseling vocation, the greater the risk of that person crossing a sexual boundary. Midlife is a particularly vulnerable time when vocational uncertainty and waning sexual drives combine. Congregations and clergy have been particularly unwilling to explore this issue due to the belief that a call to ministry is a lifetime commitment. The presumption that one must have an unwavering loyalty to this call has kept many clergy from exploring alternatives. When the call becomes a sentence, clergy are at risk for acting out behavior.

When Clergy Become Depressed

Many different emotional and physiological conditions lead to depression. People of faith have looked on depression as a spiritual malaise. Jungian theory sees depression symbolically, as a longing of the heart to be filled and as emptiness in search of God.[1] This perspective is valid, but people of faith sometimes mistakenly view depression as a lack of faith in God or a lack of trust in God's healing. These attitudes are damaging to a person who is depressed. Depression often has a spiritual component, but it is also biochemical, cognitive, and behavioral in its etiology. While it may be expressed as a spiritual crisis, it may be about something altogether different.

In a medical model, depression is viewed as the depletion of brain chemicals. Physicians administer tests to determine levels of hormonal and thyroid functioning and blood sugar, all of which can be contributing factors. Depression can be difficult to diagnose, however. The depressed person may appear to be irritable, impatient, or frustrated. Signs and symptoms include weight change, a change in sleep pattern, and a decreased ability to enjoy things that previously brought pleasure. The thinking of a depressed person may appear to be exaggerated and polarized, and feelings can fluctuate wildly or become flat. Difficulty concentrating is often a prominent symptom. The increased use of alcohol or drugs can also be a way to self-medicate during a time when depression could be cured if the alcohol use was controlled.

Clergy are more likely to violate sexual boundaries during times of depression. The depression itself and medications used to treat it can result in a lack of libido. When the pastor is feeling low and impotent, a parishioner's attention and idealization of the pastor can be a powerful antidote, and the temptation to pursue a powerful attraction and sexualized behavior with a new partner is greatest when the pastor is depressed. Sexual attractions and sexual activity increase the release of the very same brain chemicals that are replicated with antidepressant medications. The excitement and arousal of a new relationship starts all of those pleasant biochemicals coursing through the body and into the depleted areas of the brain.

When Venita began feeling depressed, she thought she was just burned out and frustrated with her overly critical congregation. She had decided to devote her life to God over 20 years before, but because it had happened so long ago, or because she was depressed, she could not remember her call or describe what it was that compelled her to enter pastoral ministry. It appeared that she was in a spiritual slump, but she had underlying medical issues that went undiagnosed. She thought that her low spirits were also related to her marriage, which seemed to be going nowhere. Her husband grew critical of Venita's low spirits and lack of participation in life. The angrier he grew, the more she withdrew into her depressive isolation. She thought her life consisted of nothing but obligations at work and at home. She believed she had disappointed everyone around her. Usually a hopeful person, she became decidedly pessimistic.

It was in the midst of this condition that Henry, a member of the congregation she served, was elected to a key lay leadership role. He offered to take Venita out to lunch to plan upcoming activities for the church. He was enthusiastic about the new programs that they created together. He bought her lunch and renewed her belief that the congregation could grow, get over its limitations, and be successful under their combined leadership. Venita saw him as the source of her hope. Henry saw Venita as an incredibly soulful person who was on a spiritual journey to find herself and reconnect to God. Her passion for God and for the church made her more appealing to him. Henry was flattered that she shared her doubts with him, and he could see that she responded to him with a spark of life when they were together. They both interpreted the energy and enthusiasm they shared as an attraction to each other, and romantic fantasies began to invade their thoughts. Once these began to appear, the relationship was set to become sexual.

Venita could have stopped this situation from getting out of hand early in the process, but she didn't. She crossed several boundaries. She met him over lunch rather than at her office, and she let him pay for the meals, so these encounters resembled dates. They met at a quiet restaurant with a private table. When they met at the church, they chose times when no one else was around the building. As soon as she felt the sexual energy and lift that this relationship was bringing her, Venita could have chosen to limit contact and stop sharing her innermost feelings. She could have told Henry that it was time to include others in their ideas and plans and that she wanted to meet with him and other key leaders next time they met. She needed to share the situation with a counselor or colleague as well.

Venita's depression limited her ability to know that she was using Henry to lift her spirits. She was desperate for good feelings. Instead, the relationship continued to develop and grew sexual over several months. Nearly a year later, with her marriage in crisis, she was reassigned to a congregation a day's drive away. When she visited a doctor in her new community, the doctor tested her thyroid levels and found the physiological cause of her changed condition. She was diagnosed with an underlying low thyroid condition that contributed to her overall lack of energy, emotional state, and level of anxiety and depression.

If Venita's congregation had spoken to her about what they saw, she might have been treated sooner. A member of the congregation saw Venita and Henry at lunch and thought the scene looked or seemed like something more than a business lunch, but she did not bring it up with Venita. She missed the opportunity to disrupt the denial cycle that accompanies a sexual fantasy.

Members of congregations need to speak up when something does not look right to them. I have sometimes heard people say that their pastor's sermons seem depressed. When I have asked if the pastor could, in fact, be depressed, they have said, "Oh, I think he's always like that." In workshops, laity will often confide in me that they are uncomfortable about a relationship between their pastor and someone in the parish that seems overly flirtatious or sexualized. Sometimes I ask, "Would you bring that up with the pastor and someone on the personnel committee?" Invariably, the person responds, "Oh, no. I wouldn't want to hurt anyone's feelings. Maybe I'm making it up." I encourage them, nevertheless, to talk honestly to their pastor.

Congregations should also strongly encourage their pastors to take time off for pleasurable activity, for family relationships, and for stress reduction. A healthy diet and regular physical exercise are crucial. A recent study reported by the American Medical Association showed that Prozac used to treat depression was less effective than regular physical exercise, both during treatment and over the months following it.[2] Corporations have found that they have more productive, less depressed workers if they encourage them to take time for fitness activity. A proactive congregation will buy its pastor a membership to a health club and tell him or her to come in late two or three mornings a week after going to the club.

> *For Personal Reflection*
>
> When have you experienced depression? Has anyone you are close to experienced depression? What were some helpful ways that people intervened or offered assistance? What were some unhelpful ways?

Vocational Doubt

Clergy (and others in a need of a vocational change) may exit the church by having an affair or crossing a sexual boundary. Pastors have used affairs as exit strategies. A Catholic priest admitted to me that it would be less shameful to have had sex with a woman in the parish than it would be to leave the ministry. This reality, as shocking as it is, helps us to see the power of the call and accompanying guilt about thoughts of leaving the vocation of pastoral ministry.

Clergy peers and members of congregations need to create a space for clergy to talk about their initial call and their ongoing discernment about it. Clergy also need to be aware that sometimes they might be called to a new vocation, either gradually or with a sudden thrust toward new education or a new career.

I wonder how often congregations have refused a pastor time off because of the financial cost of hiring someone to cover preaching and pastoral care or out of their fear that everything will fall apart in the pastor's absence. These literal costs are nothing compared to the cost of a pastor who exits the ministry, or the cost to a person who has become the pastor's lover or the cost to a child who has been violated.

When people in professional vocations become stale or bored at work, an effective supervisor intervenes to provide new and stimulating job opportunities. For example, a manager may move to a new department, go back to school for new training to implement new programs, or be given additional responsibility for the supervision of others. Within our congregations there has been too little dialogue between clergy and personnel committee members about the variety of ways to enhance the pastor's professional satisfaction. Congregational resistance to new ventures involving new leadership roles for clergy leads to clergy frustration and malaise. When a pastor asks to develop a new program, go back to school, or delegate certain responsibilities to laity, committees need to enter the dialogue with willingness and enthusiasm so that the pastor can be fully successful for the long term.

Judicatory leaders, therapists, consultative colleagues, and personnel committees should encourage the pastor to take time to reflect on these issues using paid sabbatical leaves, counseling, and vocational exploration. Career testing and guidance, often provided at the start of the pastor's call to ministry, can be helpful at various times of vocational questioning or ineffectiveness. Counseling services can confidentially address the vocational issue, especially in midlife when pastors are most at risk of crossing a sexual boundary. The cost of one lawsuit that results from a sexual boundary violation ought to be considered when the pastor asks for time off for renewal, or for career reflection. The benefits will include a renewed and healthy pastoral leader and parishioners whose relationships with the pastor are safe and professional.

Guidelines for Maintaining Professional Boundaries

Counseling

- Provide counseling within the limits of your specific training and under supervision.
- Know when to refer parishioners to professionals and get to know some of the counselors in your area so you can make effective personal referrals.
- Counsel individuals only in your professional office setting, during regular hours, and when someone else is present in the building.
- On marital issues counsel both spouses together (except where domestic violence is determined), and refer each individual or the couple to a professional counselor.
- When making pastoral home visits to individuals who live alone, take someone with you.

Sexual Feelings

- Be aware of your own sexual feelings and attractions for congregants, staff, and employees.
- Discuss these feelings with a trusted professional colleague or supervisor.
- Do not discuss your sexual feelings or attraction with the object of these feelings or with others who might be affected.
- Do nothing to act on the feelings, even if something is initiated by the other person.

Self-Care

- Provide for your own physical, emotional, sexual, and spiritual needs: time off, educational leave, family vacations, personal or marital counseling, spiritual direction, and so forth.
- Develop a circle of close friends and colleagues.
- Avoid overwork, which leads to burnout. If needed, redefine your job description.
- If you begin to believe you are ineffective, burned out, or no longer the right person for the job, consult someone you trust to discuss your vocational issues.

Dual and Multiple Relationships

- Be aware of multiple, conflicting relationships (relationships in which you have more than one identified role).
- When you become aware that you are in roles that entangle you emotionally with someone, discuss the situation with a professional colleague or supervisor.
- Establish clear expectations and boundaries with people with whom you have dual relationships.

Professional Support

- Maintain an ongoing relationship with a professional consultant or supervisor.
- Make use of available in-service or continuing education opportunities.
- Attend continuing education workshops on burnout, confidentiality, boundary setting, dual relationships, and professional ethics.
- Regularly maintain connections with colleagues in ministry.

NINE

Policies That Protect

Protecting the weak or vulnerable is an ethical and scriptural value. In communities of faith, this value is supported by the development of organizational policies that outline professional and volunteer responsibilities. State and federal laws provide additional protections by mandating that people who work with children, elders, and disabled persons report suspicious circumstances and actual signs of abuse to law enforcement and protection agencies.

Abuse and neglect includes physical abuse, unlawful corporal punishment or injury, general and severe neglect, sexual abuse, sexual assault, exploitation, willful cruelty or unjustifiable punishment, and emotional maltreatment. In most states, child abuse includes the exposure of children to pornographic materials in the home, and the child's observation of spousal abuse. Laws define the age of consent and determine whether or not a minor who engages in sexual activity is being exploited. Laws define the difference between sexual abuse and consensual sexual activity, and these definitions are different from state to state. State laws also prohibit the sexual abuse of elders and those with mental or physical disability.

How can a congregation establish its own policies and procedures so that clergy, staff, and volunteers are all fully trained to recognize and stop harassment and other forms of sexual abuse? How can a congregation protect itself from either failing to notice, or failing to report, incidents? Three policies presented in this chapter include ethical guidelines for ministry professionals, sexual misconduct policies, and sexual harassment policies. They establish clear expectations for the behavior of clergy, staff, and volunteers in their relationships with one another and with the congregation's members and constituents. Procedures regarding child, elder, and disabled person's abuse (that coincide with state and federal regulations) are placed into a fourth policy, which will be addressed in chapter 10. All four of these documents should be part of every congregation's personnel handbook and should be regularly updated.

Four Policies That Protect

The first policy a congregation needs to develop is an *ethics policy* for ministry professionals (clergy, lay staff members, and volunteers who serve as ministers). An ethics policy is a set of ethical standards that details the professional's responsibilities to those served, other professionals, the congregation as a whole, the profession itself, and the community at large. The sample ethics policy (see "Ethical Standards for Ministry Professionals" on page 136) has been developed after reviewing policies for school professionals, social workers, chaplains, and licensed counselors.

The second policy needed in every congregation is a *sexual misconduct policy* for clergy. Sexual misconduct policies are narrower than general ethical guidelines and define the professional role, elaborate power dynamics, describe dual relationships, and establish boundaries for dating and sexual relationships. Most, but not all, sexual misconduct policies are provided for congregations by denominational agencies and boards responsible for the ordination and licensure of clergy. Sexual misconduct policies define chargeable offenses, outline complaint and adjudication procedures, and establish consequences for sexual misconduct, which for clergy may include suspension or revocation of ordination.

Sexual misconduct policies for clergy often do not apply to lay staff or volunteers because denominations do not generally have the power to credential laity or revoke the credentials of laity who engage in abusive behavior. Therefore, each congregation needs a third policy—a *sexual harassment policy* that applies to clergy, all paid staff, and volunteers. This policy defines ethical behavior and includes procedures for handling complaints, remedial actions, and grounds for dismissal.

Finally, in chapter 10, you will learn how to create a congregational policy that outlines *abuse-reporting procedures* in accordance with local, state, and federal guidelines. State laws require reporting the neglect and abuse of children, seniors, and individuals with mental illnesses and physical disabilities. Guidelines and procedures need to be in writing and given to staff and volunteers who teach, counsel, and hold other programmatic roles in the congregation that serve children, seniors, and disabled adults.

The policies listed above, along with personnel policies, job descriptions, and insurance policies, provide a layer of protection for the congregation. When individuals are charged with offenses in congregations, the entire congregation is liable if it is determined that the congregation as a whole failed to inform the individual of his or her ethical and legal mandates. If an employee had not been trained to act ethically and legally, he or she could claim that the employer was at fault. If abuse occurs in the congregation, the congregation as a whole needs to feel that every effort had been made to protect children and vulnerable adults. As in a family where abuse has taken place, there is one (or more) primary victim who suffers most intensely. But the family as a whole suffers the guilt and shame of having failed in its duty to protect the innocent.

These policies protect the organization as well as vulnerable individuals within the congregation. Through careful screening in the hiring process, and through initial contacts with new staff, the expectations of professionals and volunteers are made clear to them. Stating that every venue in which staff work will be respectful and abuse free will reduce the risk of abuse. Saying "we will not tolerate abuse" will not stop every situation that could occur, but it will greatly reduce the number of incidents. Clearly describing words and behaviors that will not be tolerated helps everyone to become aware of even small actions that could escalate if not named as inappropriate and stopped.

Your congregation, I hope, has already developed a personnel handbook that defines contracts, workdays, salaries, vacations, and termination procedures.[1] If so, it will be easy to add these new suggested policies. A personnel committee, staff-parish relations committee, or other designated committee can expand existing policies and create new ones. The first step is to review professional ethics guidelines and denominational guidelines for clergy conduct. The second step is to research state laws regarding abuse reporting and definitions of sexual abuse and harassment in the workplace.

In addition to becoming familiar with laws, the committee may want to become familiar with what is called "the standard of practice" or "the usual standard of care," which means the ways that other nonprofit organizations or congregations in your area handle similar situations. In litigation regarding harassment or other forms of abuse, lawyers, judges and juries take into consideration the question of whether or not your staff or the congregation as a whole has acted normally or reasonably. They also consider whether or not you have acted within the standard of practice for similar organizations.

For Personal Reflection

Does your congregation have any policies related to sexual harassment or abuse? If so, when were they last updated? Who in the congregation drafts, reviews, and approves these policies? If no policies have been developed, what is a first step you could take to putting such policies in place?

Making Policies Work for Your Congregation

All policies need to be updated annually. When a congregation's board or trustees establishes policies regarding ethical conduct, these votes need to be recorded in the minutes of the meeting. A proactive congregation will borrow copies of policies from other congregations and review them to be sure that every area of protection has been considered. They will make policies available to the whole congregation in a newsletter and have them available at worship. Additionally, the policies should be attached to every job description for clergy, paid staff, and volunteers.

At the time of hiring, and annually thereafter, clergy and paid lay staff should be given a form to sign in which they indicate that they have read all of the policies and agree to act in accordance with them. Volunteers who work with vulnerable populations should also be asked to read the policies and sign a form indicating that they have read them and agree to comply with them. Forms also need to be signed by volunteers who work as lay ministers and make one-to-one contact with people in their homes or in other settings.

Many congregations take the additional step of requiring members who work with children, seniors, and disabled individuals to be fingerprinted and to have background checks. Workers in childcare centers are usually required to do this in accordance with local, state, and federal laws, along with all paid employees at the facility during program hours (including pastors, office administrators, and custodians). Clergy can set a good example by going through the fingerprint and background check process upon arrival in a new congregation and then can ask that others on staff follow suit. In many areas this service is free of charge. In others, there is a fee for fingerprinting, which may or may not include the background check. The cost need not be a limiting factor in any case. Some congregations ask teachers and other volunteers to pay for the process as well as complete it. When the congregation pays these fees as part of the expense of running the program, it conveys the commitment of the congregation to risk management. When expectations are high and positive, most people will be understanding and appreciative.

A congregation where every paid staff member and volunteer has been screened, where they have been trained in abuse identification and reporting, and where this information is communicated to members and visitors will be a place of safety and welcome. Visiting parents will be reassured that your congregation has taken all necessary steps to ensure that a safe environment exists for their children. Family members who bring their beloved parents to senior meals will also know that they can trust your congregation's care.

An Ethics Policy for Ministry Professionals

A sample ethics policy is included here for your congregation. Depending on your congregation's cultural background, values, and experience with abuse, this policy can be revised. The ethics policy your congregation develops is a working document and should always remain a working document. In addition to the principles established within it, your congregation may wish to add to the end of the document a statement describing procedures for filing and defending complaints, along with sanctions.

Ethical Standards for Ministry Professionals

A Sample

The Preamble

Laity and clergy who engage in the professional activities of prayer, counseling, biblical interpretation, spiritual advice, consultation, and advocacy have carried out these services for centuries, believing that compassionate service is an expression of God's love. Characterized by an appreciation for all people as God's children and for their diverse cultures, beliefs, and experiences, the work of ministry professionals includes a commitment to ethical behavior. Although an ethical code is not a legal document, these guiding principles establish the expectations of professional conduct in this congregation.

Ethical Standards

The following ethical standards are relevant to the work of clergy, lay paid staff, and volunteers serving as ministry professionals within the congregation. These standards address the ministry professional's responsibility to members and constituents of the congregation, the ministry professional's obligation to maintaining professional competence, including continuing education and self-care, and the ministry professional's ethical responsibilities toward the congregation, colleagues, and the community.

A. The purpose of the ministry professional's contacts with members and constituents of congregations is to promote spiritual, mental, and interpersonal health.
B. Ministry professionals treat all people with respect, acceptance, and dignity, and they avoid saying or doing anything that would harm the individuals they serve.
C. Ministry professionals discuss with individuals and groups they serve the purpose, goals, and nature of the helping relationships, including limitations of the proposed relationship.
D. Ministry professionals inform the congregation and individuals within the congregation of their education, training,

and areas of competency in the helping relationship. They inform individuals with whom they are entering a counseling relationship of their background, training, and competency. They know the limit and scope of their professional knowledge and offer services only within their knowledge and skill base.

E. Ministry professionals obtain regular training to increase their skills and to keep their education current, especially in the areas of professional ethics and abuse prevention.

F. Ministry professionals protect individuals they serve by maintaining records and conversations in a confidential manner. They respect each individual's right to privacy and confidentiality except when such confidentiality would cause harm to the client or others, when denominational policies state otherwise, or under stated conditions such as those covered by local, state, or federal laws. Professionals inform those they serve of the limitations of confidentiality before establishing the helping relationship.

G. Ministry professionals are aware that in their relationships with members and constituents of the congregation, power and status are unequal. They acknowledge that they have power over others as they serve as spiritual guides and mentors.

H. Ministry professionals recognize that dual or multiple relationships increase the risk of harm to those who are served, including the possibility of exploitation and sexualized relationships. Ministry professionals seek consultation as necessary to examine areas in which they may be compromised in their ability to provide services, for example, when dual or multiple relationships exist within the helping relationship.

I. If for any reason the ministry professional's level of functioning is impaired due to declining emotional or spiritual well-being, they will seek consultation. The ministry professional, along with the consultant, will determine the level to which competency is impaired and may redirect or limit the current workload until full functioning is restored. This may include the referral of parishioners to other helping professionals.

J. Ministry professionals do not engage in sexual relationships with members or constituents of their congregations or other organizations they directly serve. They do not engage in counseling relationships with people with whom they have previously had sexual relationships. They do not have sexual relationships with persons whom they have previously counseled. It is the ministry professional's responsibility to establish that no harm would result from establishing a personal relationship in the years after any form of professional relationship has ended.

K. Ministry professionals adhere to denominational and congregational policies regarding sexual abuse and harassment and all local, state, and federal guidelines regarding the reporting of neglect and abuse.

L. Ministry professionals seek consultation and supervision when assisting individuals with mental health issues. They refer members and constituents of the congregation to therapists and other professionals when the individual's issues are beyond the ministry professional's level of education, training, or competency.

M. Ministry professionals do not engage in sexual harassment of any kind with members of their congregations, colleagues, ministry candidates, or others whom they supervise.

N. Ministry professionals respond to unethical behavior of colleagues by talking directly with the colleague and, if no resolution occurs, may report the colleague to a ministerial supervisor, bishop, or ordination committee.

O. Ministry professionals are aware of the public nature of their profession and their responsibility to uphold the integrity of the faith community in which they serve with the highest possible ethical standards. They use their education and professional standing to improve the community and society in which they work and live.

P. Ministry professionals uphold ethical standards, comply with professional requirements, and agree to take responsibility for their behaviors. They do not engage in conduct that compromises their professional responsibilities or reduces the public's trust in the profession.

Professional Conduct

When asking ministry professionals to be aware of their behavior and its effect on others, congregations may find it difficult to define workplace behavior. Other workplaces outline appropriate on-the-job conduct for time spent at the office. Clergy, however, are on the job at the office, at the hospital, at the school football game, and in the grocery store when talking with parishioners. Most congregations think that their pastor's work extends throughout the day, evening, and into the wee hours of the morning, and that the pastor's behavior must be exemplary at all times and in all locations.

What expectation does the congregation have about the pastor's behavior in the community? Is there an expectation that the pastor's after-hours life be of high moral and ethical standards? If so, are there specific activities that would be unacceptable?

At a recent workshop (and in chapter 2) I told the story of a pastor whose truck was parked at an adult video store. I asked the group to talk about the rumors that might result from this. I expected that the participants would struggle with the question of how to tell the pastor they had seen his car at the video store. Instead, a group of young-adult participants raised an even tougher question: "What's the problem with it, even if he was buying or viewing pornographic videos?"

People's views about accepted moral behavior during the pastor's hours outside of the office will be quite different depending on the generation, culture, and geographic location of each congregation. How would the pastor going to a bar be viewed in your congregation? Under what circumstances would the pastor dating a person who is not a member of the congregation be acceptable? If the pastor's car is parked somewhere that is seen as inappropriate, what right or obligation does a congregational member have to be concerned?

Public ministry holds certain liabilities that are rarely discussed. The conversations that lead to the development of an ethics policy can increase clarity for the congregation and the ministry professional. If certain behaviors are expected, it is only fair to let everyone know about those expectations. As awkward as these subjects can be, it will be best to discuss them prior to any perceived or real violations of the congregation's standards.

Ministry professionals can and do make decisions about their conduct based not only on written policies but also on community standards and the value of honoring the profession as a whole. They ask ethical questions such as the following:

- Who is my primary concern?
- What are the standards of professional behavior for other professions in this community?
- How does my behavior contribute to the overall good of the congregation?
- How might this behavior diminish my own sense of moral integrity in the community I serve?

Clergy and lay staff need to be asking themselves these questions and need to be in consultation with others on a regular basis.

An ethics policy provides a statement about professional obligations to the community and to the profession itself. While most congregations have expected certain behaviors of their clergy when they are out in the community, few have spelled out these expectations or placed them in policy statements. Ministry effectiveness that is evaluated based on unspoken rules leaves clergy confused and often stigmatized. On the other hand, a proactive congregation will make its expectations for appropriate conduct known.

The above sample ethics policy also includes a section on professional impairment that may be new to most congregations reviewing these issues. Professional impairment can result from a ministry professional's prolonged exposure to loss or trauma, overwork, enmeshment, codependency, or interpersonal conflicts at home or in the parish. In the sample ethical standard, I have described impairment as "declining emotional or spiritual well-being" and "impaired competency." When ministry professionals whose personal problems, legal problems, substance abuse, or mental health issues interfere with their professional judgment or performance, they seek consultation, inform their supervisors (possibly a judicatory superior), consult with the personnel committee of the congregation, and seek professional help. They also make adjustments in their workloads, refer people to other community resources for help, and take all steps necessary to avoid harming members of the congregation.

Ministry professionals must be vigilant about self-care—physically, emotionally, sexually, relationally, vocationally, intellectually, and

> *For Personal Reflection*
>
> How does or could your congregation encourage clergy or other leaders to take good care of themselves? How has the congregation encouraged pastors and lay leaders to take time off, or checked in to see how the workload is going? What responsibilities could members of the congregation take on to lighten the load from time to time?

spiritually. Key questions that ministry professionals need to ask in times of stress include the following:

- Is my personal life satisfying?
- Do I have sexual fantasies about anyone in my congregation or on the staff?
- Can I admit to others that I need help right now or that I am making mistakes due to my limitations or current level of fatigue?
- Do I have a clergy colleague, therapist, spiritual director, or other confidant with whom I can consult to be sure that my personal issues do not interfere with my congregational leadership?

These are also questions that personnel or pastor-parish relations committees can ask pastors at various times throughout the year and in times of increased stress.[2] The pastor can be asked to consider his or her emotional, cognitive, and behavioral responses to stress at times of significant deaths, the end of a relationship in the pastor's life due to death or divorce, or a conflicted situation in the congregation. It is the job of the congregation and the ministry professional to notice and address issues of job fatigue and burnout. When good self-care is expected of clergy, staff, and volunteers, issues of concern can be raised and addressed.[3]

Clergy Sexual Misconduct Policies

Each denomination has a board or committee with the power to ordain and to revoke the ordination of clergy. Most denominations have developed policies on clergy sexual misconduct (also called "policies on clergy misconduct of a sexual nature"). The clergy sexual misconduct policy usually includes a statement of purpose, a statement of theology (beliefs), definitions of terms including *misconduct* and *harassment,* and a statement of practical application. It may also include statements about steps to be taken to report misconduct, the procedures for charges, trials, and possible consequences. Also, every policy needs to include the protection of victims and the care of those who have been wounded.

What is clergy sexual misconduct? The following is one definition:

> Misconduct of a sexual nature within the ministerial relationship is an abuse of the power of the clergy role. Such misconduct may include sexual abuse, sexual assault, sexual exploitation, and sexual harassment. Clergy misconduct of a sexual nature also includes some relationships between so-called consenting adults when they occur in the context of a clergy person's professional role.
>
> Misconduct of a sexual nature within the ministerial relationship occurs when a person within a ministerial leadership role engages in inappropriate sexual contact, or inappropriate sexualized behavior with a congregant, client, employee, student, staff member, coworker, colleague, or volunteer. Misconduct of a sexual nature within the ministerial relationship involves a betrayal of sacred trust, a violation of the ministerial role, and exploitation of those who are vulnerable. Any such misconduct of a sexual nature is a violation by the clergy person, who then bears the responsibility for his or her behavior.[4]

This definition clearly places the responsibility for sexual thoughts, language, and behavior with the clergy person. It acknowledges the power differential between the clergy person and the parishioner and notes that even when two individuals appear to be of equal status, the relationship may not be consensual. This definition carefully includes ministry professionals in a variety of roles, not just local church staff. Clergy sexual misconduct policies apply to clergy who are actively serving, who are on leaves of absence, those in extension ministries, and those who are retired.

Using a Sexual Misconduct Policy

Since the rules that govern clergy licensure and ordination fall outside of the purview of the local congregation, each local faith community needs to contact their denominational office for a copy of the clergy sexual misconduct policy. The policy for your denomination may be found on the conference or regional Web site.[5] If not, lobby to have it placed there.

A pastor with foresight sent members of his congregation copies of his denominational policy on clergy misconduct of a sexual nature. In a cover letter, he asked the members to be alert to any situations that they would consider to be violations to the policy. Before annual staff evaluations, he asked the personnel committee to check with his staff to be sure that they felt that he had always dealt with them appropriately and created a workplace of equality and respect. He demonstrated his commitment to creating a safe and respectful environment for his staff and the congregation.

Denominational policies such as this generally apply only to clergy, because those who are ordained and licensed can be held accountable for their actions through the denomination, including the filing of charges and adjudication procedures. The denomination that ordained the clergy person can suspend or revoke ordination. If your denomination lacks a policy such as this, or the policy is outdated or incomplete, work for legislative change, get together with colleagues and draft a new one, or contact your headquarters to discuss the need for it. Professional conduct policies hold clergy accountable for their behavior and reduce the risk of clergy sexual abuse.

A Sexual Harassment Policy for Staff and the Congregation

It is essential to draft a sexual harassment policy that includes paid staff and volunteers. Check in your community or county's personnel office to find a specialist with whom you can review your first drafts. A person who works in human resources usually has access to the latest local, state, and federal guidelines and definitions. Your local United Way office can help you locate sample policies from other nonprofit organizations. Samples are often available on college and university Web sites. These sexual harassment policies are sometimes embedded in personnel policies or job descriptions. They may include behavioral expectations and grounds for dismissal. Congregations that have developed policies are proud of their work and will probably be honored to send a copy to you. Once you have reviewed these materials, you may begin to adopt policies that fit your congregation in order to create a work and worship environment that is free of sexual harassment. The following policy has been adapted from the work of the United Methodist Commission on the Status and Role of Women.[6]

Sexual Harassment Policy

A Sample

Sexual harassment in congregations is considered sexual abuse and is incompatible with biblical teachings about hospitality, justice, and the obligation to treat one another with dignity and respect. Because we are created in the image of God and have equity with one another, those who participate in the servant ministries of the congregation and all who worship and affiliate with the congregation deserve the freedom to worship in the congregation and participate in other congregational activities without fear of sexualized language, humor, behavior, or discrimination. Sexual harassment is a form of sexual abuse and interferes with the congregation's ministry and will not be tolerated.

Definitions

Sexual harassment is unwanted sexual comment, advance, or demand, either verbal or physical, that is reasonably perceived by the recipient as demeaning, intimidating, or coercive.

Sexual harassment frequently includes the exploitation of a power relationship. and one of its effects is intimidation. Sexual harassment is not exclusively a sexual issue. Sexual harassment includes, but it not limited to, the creation of a hostile or abusive working environment resulting from discrimination.[7]

Gender harassment is behavior that is gender directed, denies advancement on the basis of gender, or is harassing in nature because of a person's gender. It may include either verbal or physical conduct that is experienced by the recipient as demeaning, intimidating, or coercive. Sexual jokes, innuendo, gender-directed comments on physical appearance, and pornographic pictures placed within the recipient's view are considered sexual harassment. Actual or threatened physical violence, verbal intimidation, written abuse or threats, name-calling, teasing, racist comments related to sexuality, verbal or physical harassment based on sexual orientation, and stalking are harassing behaviors that will not be tolerated.

Complaints

Members, constituents, and staff members of the congregation are urged to immediately report any harassment, abuse, or misconduct. In some instances, the conduct of concern is resolved informally by conversation between the parties and facilitated mediation. In other circumstances, the conduct is reported to the chair or other member of the congregation's personnel committee. If a complaint is against paid staff and is not resolved after mediation, and the complaint is determined to be valid by the employee's supervisor or the personnel committee, steps may be taken to terminate a job contract. In some cases, civil charges may be filed. If the complaint is against a clergy person (as perpetrator or recipient), this concern is directed to the personnel committee, the clergy person's supervisor, or the regional or conference office.

Members, constituents, and staff members of the congregation can reasonably expect that they will not be retaliated against for bringing a complaint forward. Every effort is made to maintain confidentiality for the person filing the complaint unless mandated by law or for the protection of others from harm. When a resolution is not forthcoming, civil charges may be filed. In the case that a person's conduct falls within local, state, or federal abuse-reporting guidelines, knowledge of this conduct will be reported to protective services agencies and law enforcement. Anyone having questions about this policy or the issues it addresses may contact [place here the names of the individuals or the committee who drafted this policy].

For Personal Reflection

How is staff held accountable for their language and behavior in your congregation? What kinds of professional relationships are they expected to maintain? What are they expected to do if they observe sexual harassment?

Use of the Sexual Harassment Policy

Once your congregation has developed a sexual harassment policy with the input of lay staff and the congregation, ask current staff and new hires to sign and date it, indicating their willingness to comply with it. At times of job evaluations, talk with lay staff about their experiences of the work environment and the kinds of verbal and physical contact they have with members of the congregation. Ask them to give feedback about the policy and to suggest updates and revisions as they put it into practice in the congregation.

Distribute this policy to everyone in the congregation. When anyone commits misconduct or abuse, it must be stopped and steps must be taken to ensure that it is stopped, including the filing of civil charges when necessary. Policies state the expectation that laity will be held to the same standards as clergy and paid staff.

Lay misconduct has been overlooked as often as clergy misconduct. When members of the congregation observe one of their own using sexist language or making verbal comments that demean women, touching inappropriately, or telling jokes that are humiliating to others, they are reticent to bring this to anyone's attention. Who holds lay members accountable for their behavior? When a person who has been a member of the church family for years behaves badly or creates an environment of harassment and abuse, many times friends ignore the behavior to preserve the relationship. Strong family-type bonds protect abusers and leave the pastor and even elected leaders without a means of stopping the misbehavior. A carefully developed policy would place the pastor, the judicatory superintendent, or the personnel committee in charge of dealing with complaints about any member of the congregation. Reducing the risk of abuse and maintaining a safe community depends on establishing a process for hearing and resolving complaints. Place a paragraph at the end of each of your policies that explains the process of filing, defending, and resolving sexual harassment complaints.

It's Worth the Effort

Having reviewed these three policies and the enormity of the task of putting them into place in your congregation, you could be inclined to cut corners. Don't. A custodian was recently arrested for fondling a teenager in the restroom of a midsized congregation. The family, in trying to understand why this happened, discovered that the custodian had a criminal record that no one had discovered. Not only had the congregation failed to screen the employee by requiring fingerprinting and a background check, but they had never provided anyone on staff with training or policies regarding sexual abuse. The congregation was in the awkward place of not being able to fire the custodian because they did not have anything in writing that defined sexual abuse or indicated that such allegations would be grounds for dismissal. Under the law, the custodian was innocent until proven guilty and had a right to keep his job. They had to develop policies in the midst of a crisis, and this is the worst time in which to do that. Everyone was in a reactive mode, rather than a proactive mode. So take the time and make the effort to develop those policies as soon as possible.

TEN

Abuse Reporting Policies

Our attention now turns to the protection of minors, seniors, and individuals with disabilities. A policy to cover these areas must be established in accordance with laws that differ from state to state. In addition to reading this chapter, and perhaps before you finish it, phone or visit your local protection agency to get a copy of their handbook on the laws in your state. You can also download these materials from Web sites by conducting a search using keywords such as *child protection, child abuse,* or *elder abuse.*

Congregations provide a large percentage of the nation's childcare programs and services for disabled and elderly people. Nearly every congregation has nursery workers who oversee children during worship. Most have classroom teachers and counselors for youth. All of these programs provide opportunities for adults to observe the language, thoughts, and behaviors of children. Providing safe places for those children to learn and play is crucial. Providing appropriate intervention if children appear to be abused or neglected is also crucial.

Many congregations provide services for seniors and the disabled. Meals delivered to homes or provided in the fellowship hall of the congregation put volunteers in touch with vulnerable populations. Respite care and daycare programs for seniors and persons with disabilities also daily put staff and volunteers from congregations in touch with these populations. The protection of these individuals is not only mandated by law, it is mandated by biblical principles and faith-based ethical principles.

Who Reports

Laws about the protection of children and vulnerable adults include lists of mandated reporters. The list usually includes teachers, program directors, counselors, physicians, and others. Some of these categories apply directly to volunteer and paid staff positions in congregations. Clergy and lay staff who oversee children's programs are mandated by law to report the abuse or neglect of children (or the reasonable suspicion of the abuse or neglect) to law enforcement or child protective services under local, state, and federal laws. People providing services for vulnerable adults—elderly and disabled people (including those with mental and physical disabilities)—may also be required to report abuse and neglect under local, state, or federal law.

Clergy, who have historically been exempt from the list of mandated reporters, are no longer exempt from reporting in most circumstances. If clergy obtain knowledge of abuse or neglect in a Sunday school setting, at a youth event, or in a counseling appointment with a couple, laws do not consider this information to be privileged. It is information obtained in the oversight of children, and, therefore, it must be reported.

Laws are rapidly changing, and definitions of confessional confidences are narrowing. Clergy and their supervisors need to be continually updated about laws and case laws regarding clergy reporting. For example, in many states, clergy are no longer exempt from mandated reporting laws because the understanding of clergy's confessional role has changed significantly. "Confidential communication" is a legal term referring to "a confidential statement made to a lawyer, doctor or pastor . . . privileged from disclosure in court . . . the privilege is claimed by the penitent."[1] Some state laws exempt clergy from reporting mandates when they receive penitential communication. This is an even older term that refers to a prisoner's confession of remorse for a crime. Fewer and fewer states now protect either confessional or penitential information. When state reporting laws are ambiguous, clergy and congregations need to seek advice from protective services or local attorneys about the legal implications of reporting or not reporting neglect and abuse. Once the legal implications are clear, many ministry professionals choose to file reports in all circumstances, believing that they have an ethical mandate to protect those who are vulnerable.

Other clergy choose not to file a report due to fear that they will be sued for a breach of confidentiality. This fear may be unfounded. Mandated reporters are protected under state laws when they file reports in good faith. This means that in most states a pastor who files a report cannot be charged with having inappropriately disclosed confidential information. Documentation of words or sentences that were used by someone to describe abuse, bruises, unusual behaviors, and even internal gut responses can be helpful when preparing to file a report. The language of the law is usually that the person filing the report has a reasonable suspicion. It is the not the job of the mandated reporter to investigate the situation or interrogate individuals for evidence. Reasonable suspicion and documentation suffices.

For Personal Reflection

In a one-on-one phone conversation, the out-of-state son of a parishioner confides in his pastor that he knows that his elderly mother is not eating and is refusing to answer the door when people try to help her. As the pastor, would you file a report with senior protective services about this, even if the law protected the man's confidence? Would you file a report if the law mandated it? What steps would you take to assist the family?

Information about dangerous situations is often shared with clergy. Yet for several reasons it has not been easy to convince clergy to file mandated reports. Among them are the desire to handle the situation internally and the false assumption that the pastor or congregation is equipped to handle and heal situations of abuse and neglect. Ministry professionals who do not file reports may have an exaggerated idea of their own competence to handle such situations. They may have grown up with a situation of abuse in their own family that was surrounded by taboos about telling others. They may lack the training to fully identify situations of abuse and neglect.

Some clergy are reluctant to file reports because of the perception that protective services are ineffective or, even worse, harmful to the family. Different communities have more and less effective services. Ministry professionals can increase their knowledge about what happens after a report is filed by attending training at their local protective services office or by getting to know protective agency staff. Invite protective services staff to your congregation to train staff, teachers, and the entire congregation. Working with community social service providers can also help in the first 24 hours following the filing of a report when there is an increased risk for further abuse or neglect.

Consult your judicatory and regional staff to locate workshops that teach clergy how to handle disclosures of abuse, how to think critically and ethically, and how to identify family of origin issues that affect ministry. Continuing education for clergy is one of the best prevention strategies a congregation can implement.[2]

A Deeper Look at Clergy Confidentiality

Confidentiality has long been a value for ministry professionals. How can a pastor establish trust as a person to whom others can come and talk? What would a rabbi do if, in the middle of a private conversation with a couple, she learned information that leaves her with the suspicion of child abuse in the home? Clergy of many different denominations have expressed concerns about maintaining the privacy of such conversations. The United Methodist Church's *Book of Discipline* includes a rule that clergy should "maintain all confidences inviolate."[3]

Mandated abuse reporting need not erode the congregation's trust in the ministry professional. One way for clergy to establish trust is to be clear about what will be done with information that is shared. Keeping private information private is crucial to building a healing relationship. Yet privacy becomes secrecy when others are at risk of being harmed. Every situation where the pastor is asked to keep information private or secret needs to be carefully handled. If someone is in danger of being harmed or has been harmed, this information needs to be documented and disclosed to protective services, to the individual's mental health professional, or to law enforcement.

Information about abuse and neglect cannot be kept within the privacy of the pastoral relationship without further harm to those who have already been harmed and potential additional victims.[4] For example, a teenager who was abused by her uncle disclosed this to her pastor during her first year in college. The pastor could have breathed a sign of relief that she was out of harm's way and, under some state laws, might not have reported the incident to protective services. The problem with this silence was that the woman had two younger sisters who were still vulnerable to the uncle's abuse. This is a situation where reporting was ethically and (as the pastor found in consultation with child protective services) legally required.

Secrets that are dangerous to the emotional, psychological, and physical health of others and require disclosure to protective services or law enforcement in most states include the following:

- Child abuse or neglect or the reasonable suspicion of child abuse or neglect
- Elder abuse or neglect or the reasonable suspicion of elder abuse or neglect
- The abuse or neglect of someone who is developmentally, physically, or mentally disabled
- The intention to inflict bodily harm and homicidal statements or actions
- The intention to inflict self-harm and suicidal statements or actions
- Severe mental impairment that could lead to homicide or suicide

Clergy in counseling relationships need to uphold ethical guidelines and standards of practice similar to those of licensed therapists. When a person states the intention of harming someone else and the potential victim is identified, clergy may be required (as mandated by law in many states) to inform not only law enforcement but also the potential victim. Pastoral counselors should refer clients for treatment with licensed professional counselors when their counselees have a history of suicidal ideation (plans or attempts) or other self-harming behavior, or a history of threatened or actual violent behavior.

Spousal abuse can be extremely dangerous and requires trained intervention by professional counselors. In a situation of spousal abuse, it is not standard practice for counselors to see the couple together: spouses or partners are counseled by different professionals until a situation of safety is ensured. While state laws do not mandate the reporting of spousal assault, children are abused and in danger of assault when they observe family violence. In those circumstances, child protective services reports are filed. Most clergy acting ethically would urge victims of domestic violence to report assaults to law enforcement.

Establishing Trust

People who go to a clergy person for counseling need to know right from the outset of the helping relationship that their safety and the safety of others will be the pastor's highest priority. One way that ministry professionals establish trust and protect themselves from accusations about a breach in confidentiality is to inform the congregation of legal and ethical reporting mandates. In a newsletter article clergy could say something like the following:

> I want to let you know that my office is a place for private conversations, and that I will honor what you say to me with confidentiality in most situations. However, I cannot, either legally or ethically, maintain silence when I am told that a child or vulnerable adult is being abused or is in danger of being abused. If I believe that you are likely to harm yourself or others I will also take steps to ensure safety, even if I have to break your confidence to do that.

In this way clergy can let the congregation know that while confidentiality is honored, it has legal and ethical limitations.

The Learning Curve

Nearly 20 years ago I led a workshop on child abuse in congregations at a pastor's conference. Out of 300 clergy, only three registered to take the workshop. In the past few years, thousands of people, both clergy and laity, have attended workshops on the protection of children and vulnerable adults. We are learning from our mistakes. Laity who are committed to providing safe and respectful congregations have compelled clergy to become more aware of and involved in these issues.

Congregations and denominations are beginning to require that all ministry professionals receive training in professional ethics, child and elder abuse, family violence, and sexual abuse. If clergy did not receive this training in seminary or have not updated their training for more than four years, then courses should be required as a condition of employment. Classes are available at local colleges and universities, in continuing education programs for professional counselors and teachers, and at protective service agencies.

A Sample Abuse Reporting Policy

We, the members and constituents of ____________________ [name of congregation], believe that all people are of sacred worth and that it is our obligation as people of faith to protect those who are vulnerable. [Christian congregations may wish to quote Jesus' statements about welcoming and protecting children.] We believe that it is our duty as individuals in the congregation to inform our ministry staff of any concerns we have that children, or elderly or disabled individuals, are being abused or neglected.

Definitions

[Place definitions of abuse and neglect found in state laws here.]

Mandated Reporters

According to the laws of the state of ____________, the following people in our congregation are mandated reporters of abuse and neglect: [list]. The clergy of this congregation are also mandated reporters of information disclosed to them in counseling, fellowship, and teaching, and under the law they are reporters [in all circumstances, or in all circumstances except . . .].

The Congregation's Responsibility

As members and constituents of [congregation's name], we will support our ministry professionals as they seek to protect children and vulnerable adults in the following ways:

- We will provide all ministry professionals, lay paid staff, and volunteers with education and training in professional ethics and in the specific requirements of the state regarding abuse reporting.
- We will support them in their decisions to protect children and vulnerable adults by filing reports to child, senior, and disabled services offices or law enforcement even if they are not required to do so by law in penitential or confessional circumstances.
- We also support them when they deem it necessary to disclose information in order to protect individuals from harming themselves or others.

Early in my ministry I did not file a single report to child protective services. I likely told my peers that I was serving a congregation where none of the children were being abused. I did not even know that one in three girls and one in ten of the boys were in danger of abuse, if not already abused. I had no understanding of what to look for, what signs a young person who was being abused might exhibit. I did not know that an abused child's unusual behavior was a symptom of her abuse. I did not know that when a young boy told sexual jokes or seemed to have more than a child's normal age-level awareness of sexuality, I needed to be concerned that he was likely being abused. Without education, I just did not know, and I could not prevent or intervene to stop the abuse.

After attending child protective services training, I began to identify families with abuse in them and to file reports to child protective services. It is possible that my report did not change the system, but it is also possible that it did. One day when I was filing a child abuse report with a worker at child protective services, she told me, "You have just placed the thirteenth report on this family, and I think you have given us the evidence we need to intervene . . . at last. Thank you." My call may be one call among many, but mine could be the call that protects a child from continuing abuse.

For Personal Reflection

Think of people in your congregation who could help you develop the policy on protecting children and vulnerable adults. What training do you require of your clergy, lay staff, and volunteers? Where might you send them to get this training?

Registered Sex Offenders and Your Congregation

In every community, registered sex offenders are living, working, and worshiping. Some offenses took place long ago and were committed by adults who were themselves abused as children. While some offenses were minor, others are of great significance and involve repeated acts of violence or abuse toward children or adults. Covering up any history of sexual offenses is unwise and could potentially harm individuals and congregations as a whole.

What can a congregation do to be aware of, respectful toward, and safe around registered sex offenders? Public information is available about registered sex offenders in every community. The public can obtain this information online or at state and county law enforcement offices. It is possible at any given time that there are registered sex offenders worshiping in your church or synagogue. On a quarterly basis, someone needs to check public lists of registered offenders for names of people who may be visiting or who are members of the congregation. These lists include the addresses of registered sex offenders who live near the congregation.

What is to be done once a registered sex offender is identified as part of the worshiping community? Clergy, along with members of the personnel committee, meet with the individual to discuss the circumstances of the offense and boundaries that will be placed around his or her participation in the life of the congregation. When the individual knows that public information about his or her record will be fully disclosed, he or she has no opportunity to hide.

When Stan arrived as rabbi in his new community, he had no idea what lay ahead for his congregation. Within a few months of his arrival, a member of the congregation was arrested for fondling a young teen in the women's bathroom at the synagogue during a community meal. The congregation was stunned, the family felt extremely betrayed, and the teen was, of course, the victim with the greatest amount of residual pain and shame. What could the congregation have done? Did anyone know about this man's past? Several congregational leaders were aware of the man's prior conviction for child abuse but did not inform the new rabbi or other members of the congregation. They did not want to embarrass the man or "drag him through the mud" for past mistakes. What they did not know is that pedophilia is a difficult disease to cure. Treatment involves ongoing behavioral therapy, medication, and clear restrictions on the individual's access to youth and children. Unless he agreed to limit his contact and access to youth and children, no one could ensure safety in the worshiping community.

Sex offenders who have received treatment are aware of their ongoing struggle with the temptation to re-offend. They attend ongoing support groups and individual therapy. They inform people around them about their registered status and willingly limit their access to children and youth. Sex offenders who are in treatment will be cooperative in congregations when they are asked to restrict their involvement to worship and adult study opportunities. They will also accept a congregational decision to inform everyone of their presence.

Sex offenders who have not received treatment or who are not in a healing process will be unwilling to be restricted and may need to be asked to leave the congregation. When full disclosure to the congregation is not acceptable to the registered sex offender, clergy and the personnel committee must discuss the reasons for silence and carefully consider the consequences. While it may seem unwelcoming to require that a person who is registered as a sex offender be publicly identified, consider how you would feel if you were not being informed and your daughter or son became a victim. Most parents say that they want full disclosure so that they can be part of the circle of protection for their children and adolescents.

Bishop Shamana, Bishop of the California/Nevada Conference, suggests several steps for congregations where a registered sex offender is a member, employee, or visitor. You are urged to follow them and adapt them for your congregation.

1. Inform the pastor or rabbi and a judicatory staff person right away when the presence of a registered sex offender is known.
2. Hold a meeting of the governing board to share information, and work out the details of a monitoring and information plan.
3. Draw up a plan that includes the following provisions:
   a. Designate a companion who is not a family member to accompany the offender at all times when at the congregation for worship or programs.
   b. Establish a covenant agreement defining acceptable and unacceptable contact and facilities access.
   c. Require regular contact by the offender with family, parole officer, counselor, and physician (in cases where medications must be managed).
   d. Designate a paid staff member of the congregation to regularly check in with the offender
   e. Establish consequences for breaking the covenant.

4. Inform the registered person and family that the congregation will be told of his or her registered status.
5. Write a letter to the congregation's members and constituents about the presence of the registered person and the plan for ensuring congregational safety.
6. Pray for the registered offender and the family. Treat him or her as a person whom God loves. Support his or her steps toward full recovery.[5]

Consulting an Attorney

When developing policies such as this one, and the three that were described in chapter 9, it is advised that you contact an attorney to have them reviewed. The congregation has the ethical obligation to care for those who are vulnerable, but congregational policies need to be reviewed by legal counsel. Some conferences and judicatories have free or low cost legal services.

The advice that has been provided by this resource cannot be guaranteed to meet state and federal guidelines in your area. You may want to review all of the policies with your local child protective services office. But do not forget to consult an attorney familiar with both the law and case law regarding the reporting of abuse, confidentiality, the sharing of public and private information regarding registered sex offenders, and the concepts of privilege and the standard of practice. The cost of this review will be minimal compared to the emotional cost of abuse or the financial cost of defending your congregation in a lawsuit resulting from your failure to protect.

A Final Word

Everyone in the congregation needs to participate in child protection. The more threads you weave into a safety net, the stronger it will be. The policies that have been presented to you in this book are the cords of your safety net. The only way to prevent emotional and psychological damage in individual lives and in the life of the congregation is to start weaving. What may at first seem like an overwhelming task can be manageable if you create and update policies one at a time. Start with the largest governing body and vote to make the net a priority. Then designate the jobs to committees or create short-term task groups to research, create, and update policies.

Once you have a working draft or revision of a policy or two, provide public forums in which everyone can discuss the issues. Programs and study groups such as a class to help children and adults deal with unwanted touch, a book discussion on congregational ethics, and a study of biblical references to sexuality and sexual abuse all provide strands of the safety net. The net will grow stronger by including education and awareness in every area of congregational life.

The more you talk about these issues, the more comfortable you and others will be about them in the ministry context. I talk about sex a lot. Aside from my secret desire to be the next Dr. Ruth, I find that normalizing sexuality in congregations reduces conflict and makes it possible for congregations to focus on to their primary mission of teaching and preaching about the love of God.

So I invite you to begin. Rummage through the file cabinet, hold a meeting, call in some experts, and attend a workshop. Set boundaries about touching behavior and respectful language. Hold clergy and lay staff accountable for using their roles of power to create safety in every area of congregational life. When we are all free from unwanted touch, a joke that damages, the shame of a past abuse, and the fear of talking about our sexuality, our congregations will be places of security, respect, safety, and joy.

NOTES

Chapter 1

1. To explore this aspect of the problem, see my earlier work, Karen McClintock, *Sexual Shame: An Urgent Call to Healing* (Minneapolis: Fortress Press, 2002).

2. Sandy Fritz, ed., *Fundamentals of Therapeutic Massage,* 2nd ed. (St. Louis: Mosby Inc., 2000).

3. Patrick Carnes, *Don't Call It Love* (New York: Bantam Books, 1992), 31.

4. Michael Liebowitz, *The Chemistry of Love,* as quoted in Carnes, *Don't Call It Love,* 31.

5. Susan E. Barker, "Cuddle Hormone: Research Links Oxytocin and Social-Sexual Behaviors," *Inside Binghamton University* (September–October 1998): http://inside.binghamton.edu/september-october/29Oct98/hormone.html.

Chapter 2

1. Merle A. Fossum and Marilyn J. Mason, *Facing Shame* (New York: W.W. Norton and Co., 1986).

2. Mary Kawena Pukui, E. W. Haertig, and Catherine Lee, *Nana I Ke Kumu,* vol. 1 (Honolulu: The Queen Lili'uokalani Children's Center, 1971), 60–70.

Chapter 3

1. *The United Methodist Book of Discipline.* Paragraph 161.I. (Nashville: The United Methodist Publishing House, 2000.)

2. *Ask Before You Hug.* A Video Resource by the United Methodist Commission on the Status and Role of Women. Distributed by Ecufilm, 810 Twelfth Avenue South, Nashville Tennessee 37203.

3. Ethical Standards of the American Psychological Association (1992), as quoted in Julie Martinez, ed., *Codes of Ethics for the Helping Professions* (Pacific Grove, Calif.: Brooks/Cole, 2003), 71.

Chapter 4

1. Joy Thornburg Melton, *Safe Sanctuaries: Reducing the Risk of Child Abuse in the Church* (Nashville: Discipleship Resources, 2000).
2. Melton, *Safe Sanctuaries.*
3. *Ask Before You Hug* (see chap. 3, n. 2).

Chapter 5

1. *Responding Therapeutically to Patient Expression of Sexual Attraction.* Available from the APA Psychotherapy Videotape Series. 750 First Street NE, Washington, DC 20002.
2. Martinez, *Codes of Ethics for the Helping Professions.*

Chapter 6

1. McClintock, *Sexual Shame,* 41–47.
2. Candace R. Benyei, *Understanding Clergy Misconduct in Religious Systems* (New York: Haworth Press, 1998), 101–19.
3. Bessel A. van der Kolk, Alexander C. McFarlane, and Lars Weisaeth, eds., *Traumatic Stress: The Effects of Overwhelming Experience on Mind, Body, and Society* (New York: The Guilford Press, 1996), 222–41.
4. Gershen Kaufman, *The Psychology of Shame: Theory and Treatment of Shame-Based Syndromes* (New York: Springer Publishing Company, 1996), 110–11.
5. Ibid., 110–198. Kaufman's *The Psychology of Shame* provides further reading on shame-based psychological disorders and their healing.
6. Terrence Real, *I Don't Want to Talk about It: Overcoming the Secret Legacy of Male Depression* (New York: Scribner, 1997), 103–105.
7. Patrick Carnes, *Don't Call It Love: Recovery from Sexual Addiction* (New York: Bantam, 1998), 12.
8. *Diagnostic and Statistical Manual of Mental Disorders,* 4th ed. (Washington, D.C.: The American Psychiatric Association, 1994), 296–301.
9. Ibid., 297.
10. Linda Gounds, "Stalkers: Not Just for Celebrities Anymore; Part 2: Mental Health Professionals at Risk," *The Oregon Psychologist* 22, no. 4 (2003).

Chapter 7

1. Nathaniel Hawthorne, *The Scarlet Letter* (New York: Penguin Books, 1980), 79.

2. Statistics compiled from several denominational studies by FaithTrust Institute (formerly The Center for the Prevention of Sexual and Domestic Violence), 2400 North 45th Street, Suite 10, Seattle, Washington 98103.

3. For more information, see Will Roscoe, *Changing Ones: Third and Fourth Genders in Native North America* (New York: St. Martin's Press, 1998).

4. Anne Wilson Schaef and Diane Fassel, *The Addictive Organization* (San Francisco: Harper and Row, 1988), 57.

Chapter 8

1. Thomas Moore, *Care of the Soul: A Guide for Cultivating Depth and Sacredness in Everyday Life* (New York: Harper Collins, 1992), 137–54.

2. Duke University researchers Michael Babyak and James Blumenthal, as cited in Tori DeAngelis, "If You Do Just One Thing, Make It Exercise," *APA Monitor on Psychology* 29, no. 7 (2002): 49–51.

Chapter 9

1. Congregations that have not yet developed a personnel handbook might refer to Erwin Berry, *The Alban Personnel Handbook for Congregations* (Bethesda, Md.: The Alban Institute, 1999).

2. See Roy M. Oswald's video resource, *Why You Should Develop a Pastor-Parish Relations Committee* (Bethesda, Md.: The Alban Institute, 2002).

3. See Rochelle Melander and Harold Eppley, *The Spiritual Leader's Guide to Self-Care* (Bethesda, Md.: The Alban Institute, 2002), and Roy M. Oswald, *Clergy Self-Care: Finding a Balance for Effective Ministry* (Washington, D.C.: The Alban Institute, 1991).

4. Policy on Misconduct of a Sexual Nature, *California-Nevada Annual Conference of the United Methodist Church Journal*, pp. 216–18. Distributed by Cokesbury Bookstore, 2907 West Capitol, West Sacramento, CA 95691.

5. A copy of the complete policy of the *California-Nevada Annual Conference of the United Methodist Church* is available at http://cnumc.org/docs/sexualmisconduct.htm.

6. *The Flyer* (Fall 2001). The General Commission on the Status and Role of Women, 1200 Davis Street, Evanston IL 60201. Copies available at (800) 523-8390.

7. *The Book of Discipline of The United Methodist Church*. Paragraph 161.I.

Chapter 10

1. *The Random House Dictionary of the English Language,* 2nd ed.

2. For more information, see Marie M. Fortune's article, "Confidentiality and Mandatory Reporting: A Clergy Dilemma?" at the Web site of the Center for the Prevention of Sexual and Domestic Violence, http://www.cpsdv.org, now known as FaithTrust Institute.

3. Hariette Jane Olson, ed. *The Book of Discipline of The United Methodist Church* (Nashville: The United Methodist Publishing House, 2000), 220.

4. An excellent resource on keeping or revealing secrets is Evan Imber Black, *The Secret Life of Families* (New York: Bantam Books, 1998).

5. Beverly J. Shamana, "Open Doors, Safe Sanctuaries," *The United Methodist Connection*, the newsletter of the California Nevada Annual Conference (October 2003), 2.